Shopping the
North Carolina
Furniture Outlets

Also by Ellen R. Shapiro

New York City with Kids
*Writer's & Illustrator's Guide to Children's Book Publishers
and Agents*
Relocating to New York City and Surrounding Areas

Shopping the North Carolina Furniture Outlets

How to save 50–80% on Your Next
Furniture Purchase

Ellen R. Shapiro

THREE RIVERS PRESS
NEW YORK

Published by Three Rivers Press, New York, New York
Member of the Crown Publishing Group, a division of Random
House, Inc.

www.randomhouse.com

THREE RIVERS PRESS and the Tugboat design are registered
trademarks of Random House, Inc.

Printed in the United States of America

Design by Cynthia Dunne

Library of Congress Cataloging-in-Publication Data

Shapiro, Ellen R. (Ellen Renée)
    Shopping the North Carolina furniture outlets : how to save
50–80% on your next furniture purchase / Ellen R. Shapiro.—1st ed.
    Includes bibliographical references and index.
    1. Furniture—Purchasing.   2. Furniture industry—North
Carolina.   3. Outlet stores—United States.   I. Title.
    TS885.S484 2003
    645'.4'0296—dc21   2002012329

ISBN 1-4000-4647-5

10 9 8 7 6 5 4 3 2 1

First Edition

For Steven and Momo,
the best road-trip and life companions a girl could wish for.

Acknowledgments

This book began at a cocktail party.

Several years ago, back when I was on staff at a travel magazine, I was at a party and a twenty-something couple told the story of how they had just furnished their new home. They explained that they flew to North Carolina—where most of America's furniture is made—and bought furniture for their entire home (a small starter home) at a deep discount. They saved more than enough to pay for the trip (North Carolina is a very cheap air destination—especially if booked in advance, with specials or with last-minute Internet e-saver fares), the interstate shipping (which turned out to be less than shipping from their local furniture store), and to have a couple of thousand dollars left over.

By the time they were finished telling the story, a small crowd had gathered. Not so surprising. It's a universal phenomenon: People want to have nice furniture at a great price. So I proposed an article to my editor, Arthur Frommer, and he immediately put me on the assignment. I went to North Carolina and visited the major furniture outlets in Hickory and High Point, interviewed the owners and some experienced salespeople, checked out the hotels and restaurants, and put it all together into a miniguide to North Carolina furniture shopping. It appeared a short while later in the magazine *Arthur Frommer's Budget Travel*.

The response to the article was, in a word, tremendous. Of the scores of travel articles I've written over the years, this one received the most letters to the editor, the most e-mails, even phone calls to my home asking follow-up questions. Subsequently, it is the one that people have requested copies of time and again. It continues to amaze me that my phone still rings with friends requesting copies of "that article on furniture shopping" for themselves, friends, parents, relatives, etc. I never imagined that this would be such a hit, but in retrospect the reality is obvious: *North Carolina is the Disney World of furniture.*

At one time or another, everyone needs furniture, no matter how much or how little, how big the budget or small, for apartment or house, primary residence or vacation home. And that's the beauty of the North Carolina furniture outlets. It is the furniture capital of the United States—and the world—and almost all of the major furniture manufacturers have showrooms in either Hickory or High Point (and sometimes in both, as well as in a couple of other satellite furniture towns in the region).

But there was simply no way, through the vehicle of a short travel-magazine article, to tell the full story of the world of North Carolina discount furniture shopping. A book-length treatment was the only way to do the subject justice.

My goal—in several follow-up trips to North Carolina, where I've visited all the major stores, conducted scores of interviews, and gathered all manner of information—has been to write the first comprehensive guide to furniture shopping in North Carolina directed at the consumer. My vision was of a book that was more than just a listing of all the outlets and the brands they carry. I wanted to begin by teaching people how to buy furniture, then move on to critical evaluations of all the important stores, and finally give all the necessary information for planning a successful North Carolina furniture shopping expedition, from dining to lodging to attractions.

I hope I've accomplished that goal, and to the extent I have,

I certainly couldn't have done it alone. I'm indebted to hundreds of people who helped.

The folks at the High Point Convention and Visitors Bureau, Charlotte Young and Ron Stephens, were instrumental in helping me to arrange my itineraries and in making introductions at the highest levels of the furniture business. Thanks to the High Point Convention and Visitors Bureau for assembling so much useful data on hotels, restaurants, and attractions, and making my job all that much easier. Thanks also to the folks at the Hickory Furniture Mart and Catawba Furniture Mall for the comprehensive listings of area amenities on their Web sites.

Charlie Green and Chris Bergelin, two furniture manufacturers with little stake in what is written in this book, took me into their factories for a behind-the-scenes look at the manufacture of upholstered seating and case goods, respectively.

The dozens of salespeople, managers, and furniture store owners who helped me understand the business simply cannot all be thanked individually. But special mention must go to the team at Rose Furniture, especially manager Todd Kester and salesman extraordinaire Tim Shepard, who gave so selflessly of their valuable time in answering question upon question, sometimes more than once. The Rose team gave me unfettered access to their showrooms so as to allow me to see and touch all the furniture lines, and I owe them special thanks for giving me the lowdown on the major furniture and furnishings manufacturers. Also the teams at Utility Craft (especially Sue Snipes), Wood Armfield (Larry Chilton and Kay Patseavearous), Black's (Wanda Cox and Christina Rhein), the Atrium Furniture Mall (Judy Holcomb-Pack), the Catawba Furniture Mall (Betty Ikerd), Randy Good at Boyles, Denis Rainey, and my new friend and North Carolina running partner, Jane Earnest at the Hickory Furniture Mart—everyone was tremendously helpful in providing me with access, information, and insight.

My editor at Crown, Dottie Harris, made it possible to get

this book published, and I thank her and the team at Crown for bringing it into its final form. My unofficial, uncompensated editor, my husband, Steven, helped bang the manuscript into shape and his help, too, was invaluable. My mother and father, my brothers Jon and Michael, my cousin Jane Smith, and my mother-in-law Penny Shaw all lent moral support as well as a few choice ideas.

And most of all I'd like to thank the person who invited me to that cocktail party, and that twenty-something couple. Surely now they are thirty-somethings, but I bet they still have their furniture.

Contents

Introduction

Chances are, the chair you're sitting in (or the couch or bed you're lying on) was made in North Carolina.

More than 60 percent of America's furniture is built within 100 miles of the central North Carolina towns of Hickory and High Point. And that incredible concentration of manufacturing creates serious savings opportunities for the smart shopper.

If you're planning to furnish a whole room or a whole house, buying in North Carolina can save you thousands, easily paying for the trip—and then some. North Carolina's millions of square feet of showrooms offer reductions of 40 to 70 percent (or more) on brand-name furniture from the country's leading labels in every price category, like Bassett, Broyhill, Thomasville, Drexel Heritage, and Sealy.

But while you will save money—lots of it—low prices only begin to illustrate the overwhelming advantages of buying furniture in North Carolina. Nowhere else in the world will you find showrooms of this size and with such broad selections (as big as a million square feet or more, and representing hundreds of brands), and nowhere else will you find such an experienced and highly trained furniture sales force (it's not uncommon to encounter second- and third-generation salespeople and third- and fourth-generation furniture industry families). North Carolina is to furniture what Hollywood is to movies and Washington, D.C., is to politics: It is the epicenter, it is a world unto itself. If you talk to people in High Point and Hickory, it's not just that they sell furniture: They live furniture. The local culture is centered around this key industry. Even the gossip is about furniture. In short, when it comes to furniture, there is North Carolina, and there is everywhere else.

My goal in writing this book is to bring you the best, most accurate, and most up-to-date insider information on how to get the most out of North Carolina's furniture discount stores—whether you travel to North Carolina or not. To accomplish that goal, I have been researching and writing about North Carolina furniture shopping for the past four years. My background is as a journalist, and what I do is research. I have no personal connection to the furniture industry and no axe to grind. I don't sell or lead shopping trips to North Carolina, and I don't sell my services as a designer or a consultant. I gather the facts, and I report as objectively and unapologetically as I can. I have spent many weeks in Hickory, High Point, and the surrounding areas, and much more time than that on the phone and online following up, cross-referencing, and otherwise attempting to bring you the most reliable information possible. I have personally visited the overwhelming majority of the stores described in this book. I have conducted hundreds of interviews with store owners, managers, and salespeople; with customers; with local government officials; and with furniture manufacturers and experts. I have personally investigated many stores by contacting local Better Business Bureaus. In short, I have done my homework.

Sadly, not everybody has. There's a whole lot of misinformation and myth out there regarding furniture shopping in North Carolina, and I hope to straighten out the facts in this book. Throughout this volume you will find the conventional wisdom of furniture shopping turned on its head. Here are just a few of the most important myths that need to be dismissed right up front:

Myth #1: *You should only shop at manufacturers' factory outlet stores.* This is emphatically not true, as anybody who has tried to buy more than a single piece of furniture will tell you. When a statement similar to this was made last year on a major television network morning show, the North Carolina furniture community was in an uproar. That's because manufacturers' outlets are only the tip of the iceberg when it comes to furniture shopping in North Carolina. In Chapter 1, there's an in-depth rundown of the different kinds of furniture stores. In short, the factory outlets are great and represent the biggest savings, but only if you're willing to buy what's out on the floor and available. This is useful if you're just looking for a sofa or a chair. But if you're trying to furnish an entire room or a whole house, and you have specific style and color preferences, you'll find that the time spent in factory outlets achieving your vision (if it's even possible) rarely justifies the savings. Instead, for multiple-piece furniture purchases, you'll most likely find yourself dealing with the large-scale North Carolina furniture discounters. These stores represent multiple brands and you can order the furniture you want in the upholstery or finish you want. You will still save 40 percent, and sometimes more.

Myth #2: *You will be able to buy furniture for next to nothing.* Don't go to North Carolina expecting to get furniture for free. They're not giving it away. You still get what you pay for—you just pay less if you buy it in North Carolina. You may save thousands, but if you want good furniture, you will still spend thousands. Furniture, like an automobile or a home, is a major life purchase. It's worth spending money now for high-quality furniture that may stay in your family for a hundred years or more. Otherwise, whatever you buy will just have to be replaced in a few years anyway.

Myth #3: *You can get the same furniture in your hometown.* There are stores all over America calling themselves furniture outlets, and many of them even invoke the name of North Carolina. But they are pale imitations of the real North Carolina furniture shopping experience. Don't be fooled: Outside of North Carolina—and specifically the Hickory and High Point areas—nobody has the combination of price, selection, and expertise.

Myth #4: *The shipping costs will eat up the savings.* If you've ever paid to have furniture shipped from your local department store to your home, you'll be forgiven for assuming that the cost of shipping all the way from North Carolina is astronomical. Nonetheless, that assumption would be wrong. In many cases, shipping from North Carolina is less expensive than shipping across town. The North Carolina furniture stores ship so much furniture, so often, that they are able to achieve consolidated rates that boggle the mind. Chances are, the cost of shipping from North Carolina to your home will be less than your local sales tax. And with some high-end designer furniture, or with a large purchase, you may be able to negotiate free shipping.

Moreover, this book is not just about how to save money on furniture. It is a comprehensive guide to furniture shopping in North Carolina, from taking measurements, to planning your trip, to lodgings, accommodations, and dining in North Carolina, and more.

Finally, every effort has been made to make this book as current and accurate as possible, but if you have more recent information about anything herein, please let me know via e-mail to *ellen@furnitureinsider.com*. Also, look for updates and information online at *www.furnitureinsider.com*.

Ellen R. Shapiro
New York, New York
ellen@furnitureinsider.com
www.furnitureinsider.com

Shopping the
North Carolina
Furniture Outlets

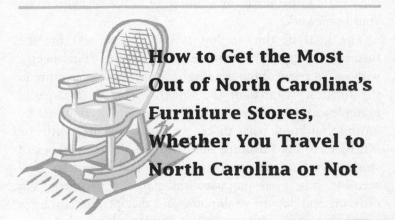

How to Get the Most Out of North Carolina's Furniture Stores, Whether You Travel to North Carolina or Not

OVERVIEW

We've all lived our lives with furniture all around us. But until you have the North Carolina furniture experience, you're like an Elvis Presley fan who has never seen Graceland, or a baseball aficionado who has never been to a big-league game. Once you shop for furniture in North Carolina, you'll never look at furniture the same way again. North Carolina is the furniture capital of the world.

Planning is the key to getting the most out of North Carolina's furniture stores. Don't think of a trip to North Carolina as an end in itself. Think of it as the culmination of weeks, months, or even years of planning. As in all areas of life, it helps to do your homework.

The goal of this section is to prepare you for the furniture-shopping experience of a lifetime. This begins with an overview of the benefits of shopping for furniture in the furniture capital of the world, including real-world examples of people who bought and saved. It continues by letting you know what to expect when you deal with the North Carolina furniture business: the different types of stores, how best to navigate them, how and when to negotiate, and how your purchase will actually proceed from ordering and deposit to shipping and receipt. Perhaps most important, this section is full of insider advice—based on interviews with the experts—on how to arm yourself for the most effective possible furniture shopping expedition: making floor plans, taking measurements and photographs, reading magazines, and shopping around locally to get ideas and inspiration. Throughout this section and throughout this book you'll find tips and strategies from veteran furniture salespeople, store owners, manufacturers, and experts, all with the goal of making you a better-educated consumer. And, of course, this section will lay out all the practical details: how best to get to North Carolina, the best times of year to go (and the critical times not to go), the situations in which you can make purchases by phone, and the essential information about airports, sales taxes, emergency services, weather, and more.

HOW MUCH WILL I SAVE?

There's no set formula for determining how much you'll save in North Carolina, but no matter what, you'll save a lot relative to the total amount of your purchase. Still, it's probably not worth traveling all the way to North Carolina just to buy a chair—unless it's a very expensive chair indeed.

To determine whether a furniture-shopping expedition to North Carolina is worth your while, you need only do a little arithmetic: First decide how much you plan to spend on furniture. Then assume you'll save from 40 percent (if you have very specific décor requirements and will be custom-ordering merchandise in your choice of color and style) to 70 percent and more (at the outlets and clearance centers, where you buy furniture directly off the showroom floor in whatever shape it's in). Then compute the cost of your trip (transportation, accommodations, meals, and incidentals) and subtract.

It readily becomes apparent that you don't have to buy a whole lot of furniture to pay for a trip to North Carolina. And since North Carolina is one of the most beautiful states in the nation, offering everything from picturesque mountains to the world's best whole-hog barbecue, think of a North Carolina furniture shopping expedition as not only an all-expenses-paid shopping trip but also a free vacation.

A simple rule of thumb: If you plan to furnish a whole room—or your whole house—you're the ideal candidate for a North Carolina furniture shopping vacation. If you're only buying one piece of furniture, it's usually not worth the trip, unless you're buying a very expensive piece of rare furniture or you're going to visit some of the many sights the region has to offer anyway: the Biltmore Estate, the Blue Ridge or Great Smokey Mountains, the North Carolina Zoo, the Penland School, or one of the many regional universities like Wake Forest, Duke, or the University of North Carolina.

To put it in practical terms, here are a few real-world examples of people who shopped and saved in North Carolina (these are illustrations based on interviews I've conducted during my research trips to the area over a period of years; some of the names and specifics have been modified to preserve anonymity and reflect current facts).

- Cathy and Josh flew into Raleigh-Durham for one day ($211 per person on US Airways), rented a car ($24.99 from Avis), did all their shopping at Rose Furniture Company in High Point, and had everything shipped to their New York home. They heard about Rose from Cathy's mother after a terrible furniture-shopping experience in Connecticut (the store was not only overpriced but also went belly-up, taking Cathy and Josh's deposit with it). Cost of trip: $475 including airfare, rental car, gas, and lunch. Purchases: all made-to-order. Not only did they save money but they were able to buy, for $800, the very same wing chair they saw for $1,270 in Connecticut, plus a lacquer secretary desk, four end tables, two coffee tables, and a complete bedroom set. Savings (including costs): $5,500, approximately 45 percent.

- Maria and Manny, a young newlywed couple, rented a truck ($66 per day), drove 13 hours to North Carolina (joining truckers for a catnap in a rest area along the way), and purchased their furniture right off the floor. Cost of trip (including three-day truck rental, gas, two nights' lodging, and meals): $390. Purchases (all floor samples): bed, chest of drawers, bureau, dining room table, and six chairs. Savings: $3,500, approximately 70 percent.

- John and Barbara, recently retired, flew down to Greensboro on Continental on three days' notice, utilizing a special fare purchased on the airline's Web site ($129 per person departing Saturday or Sunday, returning Monday or Tuesday), rented a car ($19.99/day with AARP discount), and did their shopping over a period of two and a half days (two nights' accommodations: $130, including extensive breakfast buffet). Cost of trip: $550. Purchases (combination of floor samples and made-to-order): sectional sofa, oak dining room table, and four chairs. Savings: $1,575, approximately 45 percent.

- Alice and Anne, a mother and daughter, traveled together to High Point to furnish their respective new homes: A retirement home for the parents, and a new home in the suburbs for the younger generation. Price was no object, and between the two of them they spent in excess of $70,000 on furniture and furnishings (carpets, lighting, and miscellaneous objects). They spent a lot, but saved even more: Had they bought the same furniture in the Greater New York area, they'd have spent approximately $150,000.

But perhaps more important than the raw savings, all of these customers were able to get more for their money. In other words, they were all planning to spend a certain amount of money anyway. But they got more and better furniture for that money. That's the true measure of a bargain: value. Don't be swept away by numbers. The important thing is that you get quality for your money. Furniture is an investment, and it's better to buy a few good pieces—even if they seem expensive—than to acquire a bunch of disposable junk and clutter.

WHAT TO EXPECT

Until you set foot inside the showrooms of the major North Carolina dealers, it's hard to believe what you're in for. Everything is a different order of magnitude from what you're used to at your local department store's furniture department. The stores in North Carolina are so large, so unexpected in their diversity, and so comprehensive in their inventories, it can be quite overwhelming if you're not prepared for it. Think Disney World, but bigger and full of furniture.

Hickory vs. High Point

The two main furniture-shopping areas in North Carolina are High Point (plus nearby Thomasville) and Hickory (including Route 321 to nearby Lenoir).

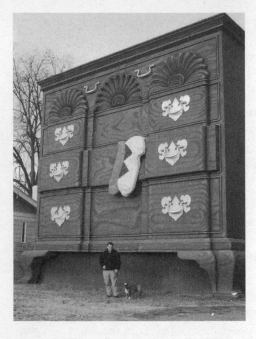

The world's largest chest of drawers in High Point

In 1859, High Point was named after the highest point on the North Carolina Railroad, and today the city draws visitors from 50 states and more than 100 countries for the twice-annual International Home Furnishings Market, the largest event of its kind in the world. High Point is home to mega-showrooms like Furnitureland South (a million square feet and growing, with so many choices it'll make your head spin), Rose Furniture Company (a much more manageable 175,000 square feet), Boyles, and Wood-Armfield. If you want to do all your shopping under one roof, with a single salesperson and in a day or two, and you're not interested in exploring North Carolina, High Point is your town: It's all about furniture. You'll need a car to get around.

Hickory, by contrast (90 minutes due west of High Point), has scores of smaller stores (though all is relative; these stores would be considered large anywhere else) collected in and around two large furniture centers: the Hickory Furniture Mart

and the Catawba Furniture Mall. Shopping in Hickory is much more familiar and mall-like, and the town lies at the foothills of the Great Smokey Mountains—a major tourism region in North Carolina. There are good hotel accommodations available on the premises of both furniture centers, so it's possible to do all your Hickory furniture shopping without a car.

In reality, you can get just about anything in either town (many of the major players have outposts in both), and prices are similar, but your shopping experience and options for extracurricular activities will be very different—and that's a matter of personal preference. If I thought one town was better than the other, I'd say so and I'd write this book just about that one town. But I've bought furniture in both places, and each is a worthwhile destination in its own right.

However, if you go anywhere besides Hickory or High Point, you're probably wasting your time. Don't be fooled by towns in other states that have relentlessly promoted themselves as alternatives to North Carolina's furniture towns. You may be able to get some decent bargains elsewhere, but the critical mass of great furniture bargains that exists in Hickory and High Point (and their outlying areas) simply does not exist anywhere else.

The Different Types of Stores: What Does It All Mean?

There's a certain image of North Carolina furniture shopping that has been perpetuated in the media and popular myth: the crumbling old warehouse full of three-legged tables and beds without rails, all strewn about and piled haphazardly. Nothing could be farther from the truth.

Imagine an entire, brand-spanking-new suburban shopping mall, anywhere in America. Now imagine that mall is just one store, and the entire store is full of premium furniture. That's what you'll be dealing with, many times over, in North Carolina.

There are three main types of stores you'll encounter in North Carolina's furniture regions:

The "Retail" Stores

Most of the large furniture stores in North Carolina are, in the strict sense of the word, retail stores. The designation "retail" is a source of much confusion, because so many people associate the term retail with high prices. Not to worry: The so-called furniture retailers in North Carolina offer prices any day of the year that would fall below the after-Christmas clearance sales anywhere else in North America.

No, by retail all that is meant in this context is that these are not manufacturers' outlet stores (see page 11). The retail stores sell first-quality furniture from dozens—sometimes hundreds—of brands. They are colossal (both Furnitureland South and the Hickory Furniture Mart are over a million square feet), comfortable, well-organized, well-lit, modern megastores with expert sales staff and even some unique amenities like video entertainment for the kids. But that's

You'll have quite a few fabrics to choose from at the large discount retail stores.

where retail ends: These stores offer tremendous discounts, ranging from 20 to 60 percent off regular retail prices—though the average usually falls between 35 and 50 percent depending upon the manufacturer and the retailer.

How do they do this? What's the trick? Actually, it's no trick: It's simple math. The North Carolina furniture retailers sell a lot of furniture. They maintain low overhead and they move product quickly. They compete vigorously with one another in a retail environment unlike any on the planet. The typical department store in your hometown likely sells just a few pieces of furniture a week, but it has to maintain expensive showroom space in prime downtown and shopping-mall areas. The typical major retailer in North Carolina might furnish a half a dozen complete homes on any given Saturday, and the stores sit on large plots of relatively inexpensive land. The North Carolina retailers have chosen to pass this savings on to you as an incentive to get you down to North Carolina. You'd be wise to RSVP "Yes!" to this invitation.

> *"Wear comfortable shoes. You're going to walk and walk and walk around the showrooms, and they're huge—hundreds of thousands of square feet of furniture. You'll walk from one end to the other, and then you'll walk back to see the table that went with the chair, and then you'll walk back to see the chair again. You'll need your feet in tip-top shape to get through the day."*
>
> —TIM SHEPARD, CAREER SALESMAN (MORE THAN 25 YEARS), ROSE FURNITURE COMPANY

It's not all about price, though: The retail stores in North Carolina afford the consumer, among other things, the distinct advantage of selection. Nowhere else will you see so many different brands displayed so extensively for you to sit on, touch, prod, and poke. On account of fierce competition among retailers, as well as restrictions and requirements imposed by manufacturers, the major retailers in High Point and Hickory are forced to carry extensive selections that stores elsewhere can afford neither to stock nor to display. In North Carolina not only is the selection vast but the furniture is arranged in galleries to simulate rooms in homes: There might be ten living rooms set up showcasing ten different manufacturers' lines, or eight dining rooms showcasing twenty manufacturers' tables, chairs, and breakfronts.

When you order furniture from one of the retailers, you're not buying the actual piece on the showroom floor (unless the floor sample is for sale, which does occasionally happen). Don't show up with a truck expecting to take your new furniture home with you. Your order, complete with your selection of color, fabric, and custom features (such as whether you want a sofa or a sofabed, a stationary chair or a swivel-rocker), will be sent to a manufacturer and produced to your specifications, and then it will be shipped to you via truck. This process can take a couple of months, sometimes more. So it helps to plan ahead so as not to get stuck with an empty room or house while you're waiting for your furniture to be built.

The Manufacturers' Outlets

More in line with the warehouse shopping concept, outlet stores have a continuously evolving and mostly random stock of furniture coming from the manufacturer. Inventory is composed of scratch-and-dent pieces, overstocks, previous seasons' lines, market samples, and other merchandise that wouldn't or couldn't be sold retail. The furniture typically is not displayed with much regard to aesthetics (it's more likely to be grouped into areas containing all the chairs, all the tables, all the sofas, etc.) and some of the stores border on chaotic, especially when inventory turnover has been high. Sales help is mostly provided to facilitate purchasing, not to assist with design and selection.

You wander the floor searching for something that strikes your fancy and then you carefully inspect it to be certain that it has no wobbly legs, that there are no scratches or tears, and to see if the price fits your budget. Savings in outlets range from 45 percent to as high as 90 percent, though one can typically expect to save between 50 percent and 70 percent on any given item on any given day. Purchases from outlets are sold as-is, nonreturnable and nonrefundable, so you need to make certain that the piece you're selecting is up to snuff. Once you put your money down, you have no recourse regardless of the manufacturer's regular retail purchase policy. (The only exception would be damage during shipping, which the shipping company will make good on; but it's somewhat difficult to document this kind of damage with regard to factory outlet merchandise.)

Most manufacturers' outlets showcase the furniture of just one brand, though some manufacturers produce more than one brand, and in some cases several manufacturers have banded together to offer their furniture in a single outlet.

Still, a given manufacturer's outlet is likely to display one or just a very few brands.

When you buy at an outlet, there is no customization involved, so you can take the furniture with you right away if you like. If you have a rented truck, you can just load it up and drive it home. Or you can have the furniture shipped to you. It's certainly more convenient to have it shipped, and depending on the cost of renting a truck it can even be less expensive.

The Clearance Centers

These stores are very similar in look and feel to the manufacturers' outlets: They are warehouse-style stores offering damaged stock, overstocks, previous season's designs, mistaken orders, and market samples, and you buy what's there and have the option of taking it home that day. But unlike the manufacturers' outlets, the clearance centers are owned by the retailers. Most of the major retailers have their own clearance centers either attached to the main store or nearby: For example, Furnitureland South has a clearance center in a nearby building, and Rose has its clearance center around the corner from the main store. Smaller retailers, like those in the Hickory Furniture Mart or the Catawba Furniture Mall, might hold clearance events in nearby warehouses a couple of times per year. In most cases, the same rules apply: Once you put your money down, it's yours regardless of the retail store's regular policy. So check carefully before you buy. Here you can expect to save 40 to 70 percent or more off the regular price.

The mishmash of furniture at a typical clearance center.

The clearance centers display multiple brands. Whatever brands are sold by the retailer—potentially hundreds—may be found at that retailer's clearance center. Thus, there is typically a broader choice of brands, though less depth in each of those brands than you'd find at a manufacturers' outlet.

For the purposes of understanding this book, even though there are differences, you can pretty much read the terms "outlet" and "clearance center" as synonymous.

Which Is the Best?

I've purchased furniture in all three types of stores. When it was time to do my whole living room, which required multiple pieces and coordination with our new paint job, I went to one of the big High Point retailers and worked closely with a salesman both while I was in North Carolina and through extensive follow-up calls. I chose the exact styles I wanted, and custom ordered them in the fabrics that pleased me. In a million years, I wouldn't have found those same combinations on a showroom floor. At the same time, I purchased a leather sofa

> *"If you find a store you like and meet a salesperson you feel you can develop a rapport with, settle in and concentrate your energies there. Going somewhere else just puts you back at square one."* —LARRY CHILTON, MERCHANDISE MANAGER, WOOD ARMFIELD FINE HOME FURNITURE

and love seat from that retailer's clearance center. It was so close to what I wanted anyway that it made the extra savings worthwhile. Had I paid twice as much, I'd have only come one shade closer to the color in my mind's eye. More recently, when I was in Hickory finishing up the research for this book, I was keeping my eye out for a TV-watching chair for the bedroom. I looked in many outlets and clearance centers, and just when I was about to throw in the towel I stumbled across the perfect chair. We threw it in the back of our minivan and drove it home to New York the next day.

In my opinion, and in the opinions of scores of shoppers I've interviewed, the retail stores are the most appropriate and efficient places to buy large quantities of furniture. If you plan to furnish a whole room or a whole house, and you have specific ideas about how you want it to look, you're going to find it hard to accomplish your mission at the outlets and clearance centers. It can be done—especially if you live in the area and can check in on the stores periodically over a period of months or years and are willing to accumulate furniture slowly—but realistically, it is not feasible for a weekend shopping excursion.

I find the outlets and clearance centers most useful for those who are looking for just a piece or two of furniture, or who are on such a strict budget that price is overwhelmingly the most important factor. Even then, I suggest that, as long as you have a bed to sleep in and a table to eat on, you're much better off buying the best furniture you can, one piece at a time, over a period of years, than you are buying a lot of cheaper furniture just to fill up the empty space. In the long run, it's no bargain.

If you have the luxury of time, you can of course combine the two approaches. You can start at the outlets and you may actually find a few pieces of furniture you really love. Then, to fill in the blanks, you can go to the retail stores where you have more control over what you'll be able to get. And since you saved so much money at the outlets, you'll have a little more to spend on the rest of your furniture.

A Note About Home Furnishings (Not Furniture) Stores

As you might expect, the incredible concentration of furniture in North Carolina has also attracted related businesses. So, while you are in town, you can also find superb selection and value on lighting, carpets, antiques, tableware, and pretty much anything else that goes in a home. Though this book focuses on furniture, I have included a section on the best nonfurniture, home furnishings stores in each area.

A Word of Caution: Let the Buyer Beware

Though North Carolina has the best furniture stores in the world, it also has some really bad ones. There's a lot of junk out there, and also more than a few unscrupulous business-people trying to take advantage of words like "outlet" and "clearance." I strongly suggest that, unless you are quite expert in furniture, or you have the benefit of the personal recommendation of a trusted friend, you shop only at the major retailers, the authorized manufacturers' outlets, and the major retailers' clearance centers.

Even when shopping at reputable establishments, it's important to assure yourself of their financial viability before plunking down huge deposits for merchandise that won't be shipped for many months. There have been some terribly sad incidents, historically, where stores have gone out of business and customers have been left holding the bag. Usually, these situations are resolved eventually, but only after a long and stressful process during which consumers may not have use of their money. So, when you finally decide where to shop, please do check with the Better Business Bureau *(www.bbb.org)*, and also visit the Web site for this book *(www.furnitureinsider.com)* for news and updates.

Payment and Shipping

Accepted Forms of Payment

In this day and age, you would think that all of the furniture stores would accept not only cash but also every credit card under the sun. You'd also probably guess that checks—especially those from out of state—would be out of the question. Well, as we all learn time and again in life: Never assume.

Credit card companies charge commissions to retailers, and even though these commissions are small (a couple of percent usually), they make a big difference on large purchases. So, for the most part, the retail furniture stores in North Carolina prefer cash and personal checks for deposits (though sometimes on deposits, credit cards are also accepted) and require the balance in certified funds (a bank check) before shipping any furniture to you.

There are still stores, however, that work on a COD (cash on delivery) basis: They accept the balance of the payment upon delivery of the furniture to your home in cash or certified funds. In every possible instance, I have included information about forms and terms of payment accepted by each of the stores. In those instances where accepted forms of payment are not specified, typically cash and personal checks will be accepted for deposits and certified funds will be required before delivery.

In the outlet stores and clearance centers, because payment in full is due at the time of purchase, most of the stores accept cash, checks, and at least a few major credit cards.

> *"Be honest and work with the salesperson. A good salesperson is going to try to interview you so he or she can best help you to find the things you need. If you're not forthcoming about your needs it becomes very difficult to give you the help that we want to provide and that you deserve."* —CHRISTINA RHEIN, VETERAN SALESWOMAN, BLACK'S FURNITURE

In all instances, it's best to cover all the bases by coming armed with both personal checks and credit cards in order to prevent an easily avoidable difficult situation. And of course, if you know where you'll be shopping, it's best to call ahead to ascertain the most up-to-date information.

Terms of Payment

The procedure for buying furniture in North Carolina involves a deposit upon purchase (either one third or one half down, depending upon the store) and the balance due either when the furniture arrives in the store's warehouse or upon delivery to your home. This half-and-half division or one-third and two-thirds division can be beneficial to the consumer, because it gives you time to collect the necessary funds in order to complete payment. Where nonstandard terms are in effect, I have listed them in the individual store descriptions.

Shipping

For those of us accustomed to paying big bucks to ship a single piece of furniture a couple of miles, it will come as a great relief (and surprise) to find that getting your furniture from North Carolina to your home can be accomplished at a reasonable and competitive price. Every retail store, outlet, and clearance center listed in this book can provide or refer you to a reliable and trustworthy shipping company. In some instances, as in the case of Boyles, the parent company even owns its own shipping company so the store and the shippers work particularly closely to accommodate the consumer. In all cases, however, the shipping companies are bonded and insured so you can breathe easy about your furniture arriving safely and in one piece.

In almost every instance, shipping will be an additional cost on top of the purchase price of your furniture. There are sometimes special circumstances under which shipping might be included in the purchase of certain manufacturers' brands or when a particular store might be running a special wherein shipping costs are "thrown in for free." It is important to remember that there is no such thing as a free lunch and that often, if a store or manufacturer is throwing in "free" shipping, the cost of the shipping is calculated into the cost of your furniture purchase somewhere along the line. I mention this not to be cynical, but to prevent anyone from making a purchase in one store strictly based on the premise of "free shipping" when the very same furniture could be purchased in another store for a lower ticket price and, when adding in shipping costs, the total on the balance sheet would read the same. You should not be scared away from buying in a store that promotes free shipping, but it is important to remember that there's really no such thing.

Shipping costs are based upon a permutation of the number of pounds being shipped and the destination to which

> *"Jump right in, get involved, put a little of yourself into the process. We're all working together to furnish the room or home of your dreams. The more details you provide your salesperson, the happier you'll be with the end result."* —TODD KESTER, MANAGER AND FOURTH-GENERATION ROSE FURNITURE FAMILY

the furniture is shipping. The more weight you're shipping, the lower the cost per pound. In the instances of the malls (the Atrium Furniture Mall in High Point, the Hickory Furniture Mart, and the Catawba Furniture Mall in Hickory), the stores within each mall work together so that purchases can be made at a few different stores but the freight charges and furniture shipments can be coordinated to best serve the customer. The best example of this is at the Hickory Furniture Mart, where not only do all of the stores use the same shipping companies but there is even a Shipping Association to best serve the consumer. If, for example, you are buying from two different stores in the Hickory Furniture Mart, you can complete the shipping information form (available at the information desks and from the stores) wherein you'll specify that you are combining purchases from more than one store. And, if your furniture is manufactured and available at different times, you can do what's known as a split ship: The shipment of the furniture can be in waves; the furniture that's ready to go can be shipped immediately and the rest can be shipped at a later date, when your order is complete. There are certain requirements for split shipping, such as minimum poundage and storage charges (though extremely minimal, in the event that your second batch of furniture is ready for shipping at different rates). Split shipping is most commonly used when a customer is buying some items off the floor (so it's ready for immediate shipping) and some custom items (usually 12 weeks but up to 16 weeks until it's ready to ship).

Please note the "350 pound rule" as well: This doesn't come up with most furniture, but furniture is getting bigger and heavier and occasionally a large piece that doesn't break down will weigh in excess of 350 pounds. In that case, the buyer is typically responsible for paying an extra fee in order to have an additional person help make the delivery. This is an across-the-board policy at the major shipping companies.

Sales Tax

If you live outside of North Carolina, and you order from one of the furniture stores in North Carolina, and you have your order shipped to your out-of-North-Carolina home, you will not be charged North Carolina sales tax. It is up to you, the consumer, to report your purchases and pay the sales tax or use tax in your local area. At present, in most states, there is no mechanism for tracking out-of-state purchases and enforcing the payment of taxes thereon, so the decision whether or not to pay is up to your personal sense of ethics.

DOING YOUR HOMEWORK BEFORE YOU GO

Shopping for furniture in the North Carolina towns of High Point and Hickory is like going to the Disney World of furniture shopping: You wouldn't just show up at Disney World without any idea of what rides to go on. A few unsuspecting people do it that way, but they spend all day waiting on lines. No, you need a game plan for Disney World, and you need one for North Carolina, too. And if you have a game plan, shopping for furniture in North Carolina can be even more fun than a visit to Disney, because at the end you get to take it with you.

The homework begins at home. I, and more importantly all of the salespeople, managers, owners, manufacturers, and designers I've interviewed, can't stress enough how important it is for you to do your homework before you make the trip to North Carolina. Of course, homework conjures up images of weekends spent at home toiling over biology or English lessons but that's not what I'm talking about at all. Your "homework" in this case is to take the necessary steps to prepare yourself for the shopping adventure of a lifetime.

You're making a special trip to High Point or Hickory because you're going to be furnishing a room in your home, or maybe a whole floor, or even your entire house—and that's fun and exciting. In order to leave North Carolina with the job done well, you've got to take some steps to make it happen *before* you leave home.

Narrow Down the Field

If you think there's a lot of selection at your furniture store at home, just wait until you get to North Carolina. It truly is beyond your wildest imagination, and better. There are so many choices it could make the unprepared shopper's head spin. That is why in the couple of months, weeks, or even days (whatever you can do, it's better than nothing) before you depart you'll want to narrow down the field and pinpoint your taste.

What styles of furniture do you like, and what styles don't you like? Do you like dark woods and formal furnishings or more casual, comfortable furniture? Think about how the furniture will be used (den, children's playroom, dining room, or perhaps the kitchen), where the furniture is going (beach house, retirement home, starter home, or mansion). Clip pictures from magazines, take photos of furniture you have at home that you're particularly fond of, browse on the Internet. In short, educate yourself. The steps you take to narrow down the field can only help to educate you and your salesperson as to what your needs and wants are. From there, the sky's the limit.

Keep a File

Start a research and collection file as far in advance as possible. Put your furniture pictures in there: Those you've clipped from magazines and advertisements, photos of the furniture you already own, and photos you've printed out from the Internet. Continue to add pictures of furniture you think you might like to buy for your home. Review that file every week or two, mercilessly tossing out the ones that you've long since forgotten and saving those that you can envision in your home for the long haul. Don't be afraid to draw right on the photos: Perhaps you like a chair but not the arms, or a table but not its color. Make notes and markings right on the photo, and train your eye to look at the individual components of furniture and not just the overall piece depicted.

Shop Around at Home

Next time you're in the mall or your local department store, pop in and check out the furniture selection. What do you see that strikes your fancy? What lacks in appeal? That dining room table is beautifully designed but the finish is too dark or maybe it looks a little flimsy for the money? It's like shopping for a wedding dress or a car: Ask yourself, how does it look (is it attractive enough that you'll want to see it every day for the duration?), how does it feel (is it going to fall apart or break down?), and will it stand up to the test of time (sitting, spilling, children)? Depending on how strict the supervision is at a given store, you might be able to take some photos of furniture you like. Also note the brand name and model number, if available, of any piece you like. This doesn't always work—some stores have private-label merchandise with nonstandard model numbers—but it never hurts to try.

Floor Plan

Ideally, you want to bring the architect's blueprints of your home so you have the true dimensions of each room as well as the layout of the house (which includes widths of doorways, staircases, and hallways). Be sure to note any changes or additions to the blueprints—like built-in bookshelves lining the living room wall or the expansion of the master bedroom. If you have the blueprints, great, add them to the file (or pile) of things you'll bring along on your furniture shopping trip.

Then again, you may not have access to your blueprints, especially if you live in an older home or you're a renter. Still,

> *"If you connect with someone the longevity factor is great. I've been here 20 years, Sue's been at Utility Craft 28 years, and some of us are on our third generation of customers. You just don't get that anywhere else."* —LARRY CHILTON, MERCHANDISE MANAGER, WOOD ARMFIELD FINE HOME FURNISHINGS

you can come armed with all of the necessary information by taking the measurements yourself—and it's always a good idea to confirm the key measurements on your blueprints anyway, because you never know if the builder executed the architect's plan precisely.

For starters, you'll want to have the dimensions of each of the rooms you intend to furnish (length, width, height). But don't stop there. You also need to note:

- Where the windows are (measuring from the corners of the room into the window), how high they are off the floor (measuring from the floor up to the bottom of the window sill), and how tall they are (from the bottom of the window sill to the top of the window or window molding).

- Where the doorways and closets on each of the walls are located (measuring from the corner to the molding or doorframe) and how much space is between them. Which way do the doors open?

- What is the width of your front door, hallway, staircase? Does the staircase make a turn? What is the maximum width at the turn and is there an opposing wall or is it an open staircase? Will the china cabinet have to go through the kitchen to get to the dining room? Are the entrances wide enough to accommodate it? Do you use an elevator to get to your apartment? Will your furniture fit in the main or freight elevator?

- Are there any special considerations in your home? Do you live in a loft and have wide open spaces and very high ceilings? Do you live in an old home with a finished attic and low eaves? Are you in a contemporary home with split levels and funky stairways? Are there any walls that can't be covered due to built-ins like bookcases or cabinets? These are questions that only you can answer and though the salespeople have heard about all sorts of special circumstances, they can't tell you what will fit and what won't unless you provide the basics.

- Where are your electrical outlets? Do you have wall sconces? Do you have a ceiling fan or chandelier that effectively lowers the usable height of the room? Be sure you note the exact location of anything you don't want blocked by your furniture.

Right about now you might be thinking to yourself: "Hey, all I want to do is go to North Carolina and buy some furniture! This is turning out to be more of a production than it's worth!" But remember, no matter where you go—even if it's the furniture store around the corner—you'll have to know the answers to all of these questions or you'll end up with furniture that can't fit through your doorway or blocks half of your window. And it's always easier, more gratifying, and more economical if you come prepared.

In addition to jotting down all of the dimensions in your furniture notebook, you might also consider laying out your rooms on graph paper (this is also something that can be done in the design centers at most of the stores). Designate a certain number of blocks per foot—maybe two to four depending upon the size of the home—noting doorways, windows, closets, and so forth, and begin to lay out the room, "placing" the furniture to scale and figuring out how you want the room to look and how much space you actually have to work with

> *"Jump in it, sit in it, use it. You're supposed to be able to sit down on that couch or that chair and there should be no surprises— there shouldn't be anything in that seat that you don't expect (a spring, a board, etc.). And hey, can you get up out of it?"*
> —CHARLIE GREENE, MANUFACTURER, CLASSIC GALLERY

once you start filling it up. Again, this can be done with your salesperson—many of whom have degrees in interior design (and most of those who don't have years and years of experience with this very thing)—but you can also take some time at home before you go to figure out some of the broader points. The more preparation you do before you go, the more fun you will have along the way, and the more time you can spend actually shopping for furniture.

Samples and Swatches

Collect fabric swatches, paint chips, wallpaper samples, kitchen tiles, carpet threads—whatever it is that you will be working with and around. You'll want to have that information with you. How can you decide on the fabric for your sofa if you're not certain about the color of your carpeting and wallpaper? Is the carpet sky blue, pale blue, or powder blue? Are the walls a small floral print with an ecru background, a miniature floral print with an eggshell background, or would you categorize your wallpaper as being a medium floral print with a pearl background? Now multiply that by all of the rooms you plan to furnish. Are you overwhelmed yet? Don't be. Instead, take steps to be prepared. Rather than suffering and second-guessing yourself throughout the entire process, you'll be able to enjoy it and get excited about your new sectional that perfectly matches the pale blue carpet and the miniature floral print with the eggshell background.

> *"The number one thing you can do to help yourself before you come is make a budget! There is an enormous selection of furniture in every price category and without a budget of some kind it's extremely difficult for the salesperson to know what to show you. Taking this one step can save you a tremendous amount of time and frustration."*
>
> —JUDY HOLCOMB-PACK, DIRECTOR OF MARKETING, ATRIUM FURNITURE MALL

What to do if you don't have the swatches, chips, and cuttings: If you don't have a paint chip from your bedroom or a piece of carpet from the den, how can you still come prepared? Where there's a will, there's a way—rest assured, there's always a way to get the tools you need. For carpeting, go in a corner, perhaps near a wall, under a table leg or under the floor lamp and clip a strand or two. No one will ever be the wiser (including you in an hour or two) and you'll have the carpet sample you need for the trip. For paint chips, remove a light switch cover—attached to the cover or just underneath you'll be able to get a color chip. If it's a Persian rug you're dealing with, take some photos (be sure to check the pictures for likeness; sometimes flash photography or overhead lighting can vastly alter the appearance on film) to bring along. The same can apply to a kitchen floor, wallpaper, and centerpiece art. The best option is to have the swatches, chips, and samples along, but good photographs will also do the trick.

Visual Aids

You have a corner where you would like to place a sectional sofa for television viewing. The corner would allow you 92 inches across one wall and 59 inches across the other counting from the corner. It seems like the perfect solution to the corner problem and allows for the most optimal seating in the room that gets so much use among family and friends. But you're just not sure. Couches are much wider these days, it seems. The one you saw in the department store was 78 inches, the one you saw online was similar. *Is the sectional sofa really going to work in that corner or will it overwhelm the room and dwarf the empty space? Or is it too small and will it be lost in the vastness of your room?*

The best way to get an idea for what the sectional will look like in your room (shy of getting it in there) is to have an arts and crafts project: Take some newspaper and lay it out in the appropriate dimensions—length and width—to see how and where you envision your furniture will go. You'll also want to remember the height (though it's pretty hard to get newspaper to stand straight up), which is very important for windows, cabinets, artwork, and anything else that might be obstructed by the back of the furniture. Holding up a yardstick in the middle of your newspaper sectional can give you some idea of the total size. It is not an exact science but it will give you a much better idea of the space you intend to fill and how you'll want to fill it. You can also trace outlines on the floor with masking tape.

It really helps to do this, because when you're in the middle of a one-million-square-foot furniture showroom—or even a 100,000-square-foot showroom for that matter—even the chunkiest furniture looks very small. But when you bring that furniture into your 300-square-foot dining room, it suddenly looks very big—perhaps too big—if you don't first know what to expect.

Photograph the Rooms You Plan to Furnish

It's always helpful to provide a visual aid of what you're working with. This can help refresh your memory (even though you live there, it's amazing how you can forget the simple details you see every day) and provide your salesperson with a little extra insight. If there is any furniture or art in a room that you'll be working around, be sure to include a picture of that. Otherwise, if you're working from a blank slate, stand in the middle of each room and shoot a picture in all four directions. You might also want to shoot the room from different angles or perspectives, then stash all of the pictures in your furniture file until you're ready to go. Photo tip: It's a good idea to have a standing person in the photos—even if that person's back is to you—to give perspective to the room.

ONCE YOU GET THERE

Choosing a Salesperson

After doing your homework, the next most important thing you can do for yourself is find the right salesperson to help you. Only you can determine who is a good match for you, but it really is critical for you to link up with someone. This salesperson (who may have a degree in interior design or decades of experience selling furniture to people just like you) is on your side. He or she wants you to be happy and leave satisfied whether you buy something or not. I can't tell you how many times I've heard salespeople say "a referral is the best compliment any customer can give me." And they really mean it—so let them do their job and allow them to help you get the job done.

You can even shop for a salesperson before you go. Do you have friends who have shopped for furniture in North Carolina? If they were happy with their salesperson, call ahead and make an appointment so you can be sure that person is available the day you roll into town. Throughout the pages of this book you'll see quotes from furniture salespeople, along with information about where they work. Do you like what they say? If so, call ahead and try to make an appointment. Or just phone the store ahead of time and say you'd like to make an appointment with an excellent, experienced salesperson for whatever date you like. The mere act of calling ahead is a signal to the store that you're a serious customer, and the staff will go out of their way to accommodate you. If, however, you don't have a tie to any particular salesperson, it's fine to simply show up and see how you feel about the salesperson who greets you because most people who are coming to shop for furniture in North Carolina come unannounced and leave fully furnished and satisfied just the same. If you like the match, great. If for some reason you don't, don't be afraid to request someone else or to try another store.

How to Navigate the Stores

Even the so-called small stores in High Point can boggle the mind with selection, and in Hickory it's important to figure out where in the malls to start and which stores have what. The first course of action is to approach the front desk when you enter the store (same applies in the mall stores). That's where the directory to the store will be, where you'll find out about any special in-store promotions, and where you can hook yourself up with a salesperson. It is critical, whether you want to work with a salesperson or not (though I strongly encourage you to do so), that you find out about the store's layout and manufacturer lines so that you don't waste your time wandering the store aimlessly.

If you're shopping the malls in Hickory (Hickory Furniture Mart and the Catawba Furniture Mall), you'll also want to be certain that you stop by the main mall entrances where there are greeters with mall directories and a wealth of information on all manner of mall issues, from shipping to specials to who specializes in what. In the Furniture Mart the main entrance is the *South* entrance, though there is also an information booth/visitor's center at the *West* entrance. At the Catawba Furniture Mall, the main entrance is the "Courtyard Entrance"

> *"Mattresses and box springs are not like they used to be: they're a lot thicker and wider. So if you have an old bed and you buy a new mattress and box spring, you may not be able to see the headboard behind the mattress. Be sure to take measurements so you can avoid this pitfall."* —SUE SNIPES, MANAGER, UTILITY CRAFT FURNITURE

between American Décor and Studio 70. If you enter elsewhere, make your way over to the information desk before you begin so you can orient yourself and get answers to any questions (even the ones you didn't know you had).

The Designer Option

If you hire a designer in your hometown, you will typically pay that person twice: You'll pay for that person's design services, and you'll also pay a designer's markup on any furniture the designer buys on your behalf. Unless you have money to burn, I don't recommend that arrangement.

You can, however, hire a designer to come furniture shopping with you. This way, you pay only for what you really get: the services of an expert. But you get to save on furniture just as if you had bought it alone.

It can be a distinct advantage to work with a designer while furniture shopping in North Carolina, particularly if you have a lot of furniture to buy. Sometimes, utilizing the help of a designer for a few hours or a few days to help you take the guesswork out of furnishing your home during whatever amount of time you have makes the trip a bit more relaxing. It's best to make an appointment in advance if you know you want the help of a designer, or even if you just want to have the practiced eye and years of experience of a professional to show you the ropes. The local designers will take the edge off and turn your shopping experience into an entertaining adventure.

It is, however, by no means necessary to hire a designer if you know what you want. I know plenty of people (no one I know personally has hired a designer) who have come to shop and in two days have furnished an entire home. These were decisive people who did a lot of advanced preparation. If you do decide you want to work with a designer, to make arrangements in advance call the High Point Convention and Visitors Bureau for referrals or one of the High Point furniture stores. In Hickory, try Designing Women in the Hickory Furniture Mart. Or if you think you might want to go it alone, you can always start out by yourself with the help of your salesperson, who may very well have a degree in interior design, some design education, or at a minimum will have been helping people just like you furnish their homes for many years—and ask for a referral once you're there.

Rates: The local designers are mostly available on a per-hour basis (with a variable minimum number of hours) or at a set daily rate. I do not make any specific recommendations (though I do mention Designing Women in the Hickory Furniture Mart because they are on the premises and I interviewed the owner, Sally Bently, at great length and also interviewed some of her clients) because I, myself, have never worked with any designers while shopping for furniture in North Carolina.

HOW TO GET THE BEST PRICES

Negotiation

North Carolina's furniture discounters operate high-volume businesses at razor-thin profit margins in an ultra-competitive environment. Thus, the negotiating cushion is pretty small. "Most discounters' prices are within a few dollars of each other on any given item," says Todd Kester, sales manager of Rose Furniture Company and a fourth-generation Rose man (his great-great-grandfather started Rose furniture in 1925).

"Extensive shopping around usually won't save you enough to justify the extra night's motel stay." My independent research confirms the veracity of Kester's statement—rarely did I see a significant difference in price on quality, name-brand merchandise.

"Competition keeps everybody honest," confirms Betty Ikerd, an owner of the Atrium and Catawba Furniture Malls. She adds, "Of course, it never hurts to ask about additional savings, especially on a big sale. But no salesperson is going to take off too much because, beyond the small profit margin, all that's left is their commission," usually a modest 4 percent.

Some experts advise, confidentially, that high-end brands like Thomasville regulate the lowest prices a discounter can charge in order to protect their images; consequently, profit margins on these brands are higher and it's sometimes possible to negotiate free shipping. Remember, in shopping, as in all things, it never hurts to ask. But don't expect the world; the prices are already very, very low.

Shoppers Discounts

Every store has some sort of yearly sales, whether scheduled annually or less systematically. As a general rule it is safe to assume that, at a minimum, stores will offer "after Market" sales, which begin anywhere from a few weeks to a couple of months after Market. Usually April Market samples will go on sale in May, and October Market samples will go on sale in November but these things are always variable based on the store and the manufacturer. See the end of this chapter—Best Times of Year to Go—for an explanation of "Market."

I have indicated scheduled annual sales at each of the stores, outlets, and clearance centers whenever applicable. There are, however, plenty of other sales of the surprise variety, where the public is not notified of the sales months in advance but rather weeks or even days before the sale event is scheduled to hap-

> "If you have the time, shop the furniture outlets and clearance centers first. You might find some great pieces of furniture at outlet prices. Then, move on to the quality discount furniture stores. The savings in the outlets and clearance centers often allow you to purchase more than you originally anticipated."
> —DENIS RAINEY, RAINEY & ASSOCIATES, INC.

pen. Some of the outlets and clearance centers have their annual warehouse sales and people come from miles around to take advantage of the super savings. In these sales the prices are scheduled based upon the day of the sale: The first day the price of a leather lounge chair might be $600, the second day it might drop 10 percent off the ticket price, and the third and final day it might drop 20 percent. Usually, at the warehouse sales, the savings are great, especially if you can hold out until the final day of the sale (which, of course, is a big gamble and tradeoff for the potential prize of the *big* savings).

Passport to Savings

Another unique and special way to save (and a heck of a lot more predictable, too) is through the High Point Convention and Visitors Bureau (CVB) *Passport to Savings* plan. The *Passport to Savings* is completely free; you just have to go online and request one, or give a call to the CVB and ask for your *Passport*, and it's yours. Although 2002 was the first year the passport was offered and many regional High Point stores and businesses participated, more and more have subsequently jumped on the bandwagon to bring the savings home to you, the shopper. Some sample *Passport* savings include a free night's hotel room with minimum purchase, split freight charges with purchase, payment of sales tax with minimum purchase, free admission for one to the Doll and Miniature Museum with paid admission, discount on local movie tickets, additional 10 percent off purchase, free "furniture shopping survival kit," hotel rate specials, discounted meals, discounted car rentals, and so forth. Each store or business has a page detailing its savings to you. If you're planning a trip, it's best to request your *Passport* early so you can plot your shopping, staying, and saving strategy well in advance.

Also see Hotel Discounts and Shopping Packages below.

WHEN TO SHOP LONG DISTANCE

Most North Carolina furniture stores accept telephone orders, so why travel all that way? Why not just browse your local department store, write down model numbers, and order by phone? Well, for one thing, to protect their retail dealers from that very thing, some brands (most notably Thomasville) will not allow the North Carolina stores to sell to customers unless they have been in the store within the previous 90 days. And the only way to shop the clearance centers and outlets is to browse in person.

As a general rule, I would advise anyone who is looking to purchase a substantial amount of furniture (furnishing a room, a floor, a whole house) to shop North Carolina in person. There is no way to grasp—and more important, to see—the tremendous selection without being there yourself. (At some furniture stores in North Carolina, the room where you go to look at fabric swatches and catalogs is, all by itself, 5,000 square feet or more.) Nor can you benefit from the expert and knowledgeable sales staff without showing up in person.

There are, however, a few exceptions to this rule: First, if you have already made the pilgrimage to North Carolina and you were unable to make the final decisions until you returned home, following up with your salesperson and placing an order by phone is an ideal solution (I have done this, and sometimes it's the best move if you need some time to think). Second, if you have previously shopped in North

Carolina and you have a salesperson who knows you and with whom you like to work, placing additional orders by phone (or via the Internet if the store accepts them) is a fast and efficient way to fill in gaps (so long as you aren't planning to buy any furniture by manufacturers who restrict remote orders). Third, if you are in need of a single piece of furniture, or even two or three, you might find that with shopping around at home, researching online (many of the furniture stores now have extensive Web sites detailing stock, though some don't allow Internet orders), or working with an experienced salesperson you can find the item you're looking for without making the trip. Finally, if you really can't make it there, the phone or Internet are viable options. Last time I was in About Last Nite, someone had e-mailed in an order from Singapore.

TRAVEL TO NORTH CAROLINA

Getting There: Flying vs. Driving

In order to determine whether you should drive or fly to North Carolina, you first have to determine a few different things. Are you on a tight budget? Are you in a hurry to have your new furniture? Are you passing through on your way to somewhere else or interested in combining your shopping trip with your vacation? Are you flexible about your selections?

If you answered yes to all of these things, you probably should drive to North Carolina (and even rent a truck). For those shopping on a tight budget, the clearance centers and outlet stores are often the way to go. The savings are greatest and you buy the furniture as is and off the floor so you can load it up and drive it home yourself (if you want to). If you aren't interested in driving a truck, unloading the furniture yourself, or driving to North Carolina, you can fly down and have the furniture shipped home from the outlets and clearance centers. Usually, it will arrive within a couple of weeks depending upon the destination.

Custom furniture (80 percent of customers order some sort of custom furniture) takes 8–12 weeks to be manufactured and up to 16 weeks from the date of order to arrive in your home so, again, if you're in a hurry and you're somewhat flexible, you can buy off the floor from the clearance stores, outlets, and even the retail stores and your furniture is ready to go home with you or ship on the first truck bound for your home state.

Buying off the floor isn't for everyone: You don't know if you're going to find anything you like and need, you may be coming from far away and don't want to gamble on availability, you have specific ideas in mind, you may have an entire house to furnish on this trip and the clearance centers are far too haphazard to accomplish that goal in one visit, or you're tight on time. If you're nodding your head in agreement, you'd do best to fly. If you're on a tight budget, you can book your flights a couple of weeks in advance. Flights out of the Northeast and Midwest into Greensboro often cost $100 or less; same goes for last-minute Internet fares that appear regularly. Flying also means you'll arrive fresh. Unless you're within a couple of hundred miles, driving to North Carolina will take a bite out of your shopping time and wear you out before you even arrive. And remember, even if you buy off the floor and you drive, you can still ship your purchases home. As long as there's shipping available (each store has its own shipping policy and contractors) there's no rule that says you have to take it with you.

Air Transportation to High Point

The closest airport to High Point is Piedmont Triad International in Greensboro (PTIA is approximately 15 miles northeast of High Point) and it is serviced by a number of major national carriers. There are more than 70 regularly scheduled flights to this airport so you should have no problem finding an airline that services your area. Advance bookings, last-minute bookings, and Internet specials are your best bet for finding rock-bottom-priced tickets. Often, from Midwest and East Coast cities you can expect to find flights in the $100 neighborhood.

If flights to Greensboro are less than ideal for your needs another option is Raleigh-Durham International Airport (RDU is approximately one hour's drive from High Point). RDU is also serviced by a number of major national carriers and roundtrip tickets regularly drop below $100 (working around the usual restrictions). Car rentals are available on site at both airports through national agencies.

Air Transportation to Hickory

Hickory has its own little airport, Hickory Regional, which services commuters on small planes, private planes, and charters. Unfortunately, the commuter service run by USAirways is no longer operating, so unless you plan to fly in on a private plane, your best (and closest) bet is to fly into Charlotte. Charlotte/Douglas International Airport is approximately one hour from Hickory and is serviced by a number of major carriers. It is also a hub for USAirways so that is a good bet for cheap tickets. As with the other airports, check the Internet for specials and book a few weeks out for the best rates.

If You're Driving

High Point is in central North Carolina on U.S. Route 311 near Interstates 85 and 40. Hickory is farther west, directly accessible from Interstate 40.

If you plan to drive to North Carolina, your best bet is to call any retailer for directions, because especially in High Point they tend to be fairly spread out so the same directions do not apply to all.

Train

High Point is also accessible by Amtrak passenger train.

Hotel Discounts and Shopping Packages

All of the big stores and each of the malls have arrangements with the local hotels to provide lodging discounts to furniture shoppers. Before you book a room, therefore, be certain to check out stores' (or mall) Web sites for money-saving referrals, and mention the store at which you'll be shopping for your discount. Most of the stores even provide links to the hotel Web sites so you can get a look at the hotel before you book it. If you're not technologically oriented, call any one of the stores you're planning to shop and ask the receptionist (or your salesperson if you've already got a relationship going) for a recommendation of which hotels offer furniture shoppers' discounts. The same applies to the malls: Check the mall Web sites or call the malls' main numbers for recommendations and referrals. Don't forget to ask about other discounts that may apply, such as AAA, AARP, and corporate discounts.

If you're interested in group shopping, the Atrium Furniture Mall in High Point and the Catawba Furniture Mall in Hickory offer weekend shopping excursions (four times per year). Each mall has its own program but the way it *usually* works is that shoppers arrive on a set date, get lodging and breakfast in the designated hotel, are shuttled to and from the mall, have access to lectures or a private session with a designer (variable based upon the mall and the specific weekend), get a coupon for a free lunch, and are presented with useful furniture shopping goodie bags (often a tote bag with ruler or tape measure, graph paper, pens, etc.). Now personally, I can't imagine wanting to shop with a group—I'd just as soon set my dates when it was most convenient for me, stay at the hotel of my choice with whatever discount I was able to arrange, and go about my business. But some people rather

> *"A lot of the stores have Web sites. Take some time to pre-shop online and you'll find that you can dramatically narrow down your interests and save yourself a lot of time and energy once you actually arrive."* —ANTHONY LOCKHART, STORE MANAGER, BOYLES FURNITURE

like the idea of a shopper's weekend and because everyone is on his or her own for shopping anyway, the group mentality doesn't really exist—it's more a matter of taking advantage of the available benefits and small extras you might reap as a result of joining a group rather than actually being bound to the other shoppers.

Important Telephone Contacts

High Point (Area Code 336)
   High Point Convention and Visitors Bureau:
      (800) 720-5255
   Hospital: (336) 878-6000
   AAA: (336) 882-8126
   Arts Council: (336) 889-2787
   Chamber of Commerce: (336) 889-8151
   City Hall: (336) 883-3289
   Piedmont Triad International Airport: (336) 665-5666
   Public Library Main Branch: (336) 883-3660
   Amtrak: (800) 872-7245

Hickory (Area Code 828)
   Hickory Metro Convention and Visitors Bureau:
      (800) 849-5093
   Catawba County Chamber of Commerce: (828) 328-6111
   Hickory Regional Airport: (828) 323-7400
   Hospital: (828) 326-3000

General
  Emergency: 911
  North Carolina Tourism Information: (800) VISITNC

Sales Tax

North Carolina sales tax is 6.5 percent.

Weather

WEATHER FOR HICKORY AND HIGH POINT

HICKORY

	JAN	FEB	MAR	APR	MAY	JUN	JUL	AUG	SEP	OCT	NOV	DEC
Avg. Temp.	38° F	41° F	50° F	58° F	66° F	73° F	77° F	76° F	70° F	59° F	50° F	41° F
Avg. Precip.	3.60 in	4.20 in	4.80 in	3.50 in	4.50 in	4.70 in	4.60 in	4.10 in	4.20 in	3.80 in	3.60 in	3.50 in

HIGH POINT

	JAN	FEB	MAR	APR	MAY	JUN	JUL	AUG	SEP	OCT	NOV	DEC
Avg. Temp.	39° F	42° F	51° F	60° F	67° F	74° F	78° F	77° F	71° F	60° F	51° F	42° F
Avg. Precip.	3.50 in	3.60 in	4.00 in	3.00 in	4.30 in	3.90 in	3.90 in	4.50 in	3.30 in	3.70 in	3.20 in	3.50 in

(Source: National Climatic Data Center)

Important Local Information

Alcohol Laws
  Legal drinking age 21
  Beverages served until 2:00 AM
  Alcohol sold in ABC stores; beer and wine are sold in
    convenience and grocery stores only

Road Laws
  Front seat belts required
  Back seat belts not required over age 12
  $25 fine for failure to wear seat belt
  Child restraint seat required for ages under 4
  Seat belt required ages 4–12

Headlights required when using windshield wipers
Motorcyclists wear helmet and burn headlights

Speed Limits
Local 35 mph, unless otherwise posted
Highway 55 mph, unless otherwise posted
School zone and residential 25 mph

Online

Nearly every furniture store and manufacturer of any signifi-
cance has an online presence, and those are listed throughout
this book as well as in an appendix at the end, along with many
other useful Web sites. There are, however, two excellent gate-
ways through which you can find the most up-to-date and accurate local information, and they are the Web sites maintained
by the High Point and Hickory Metro Convention and Visitors
Bureaus. Spending a little time on these sites in advance of your
visit will make everything easier once you're in town.

High Point Convention and Visitors Bureau:
   www.highpoint.org
Hickory Metro Convention and Visitors Bureau:
   www.hickorymetro.com

Best Times of Year to Go

There is only one bad time to plan your shopping visit to
North Carolina and that's during the International Home
Furnishings Market. Market takes place *twice each year*, once
in April and once in October. High Point becomes an
absolute zoo: All of the hotel rooms are booked up months
in advance, the salespeople are harried running around to the
different showrooms to see the latest designs and trends, the
restaurants are packed to the gills, and designers, buyers, and
manufacturers arrive from all over the state, the country

(attendees from all 50 states), and the world (attendees from over 100 countries) to view the latest in furniture and accessories. Even if you were willing to brave all of this to see the biggest furniture show in the world, it is closed to the general public so you couldn't get in anyway. Don't feel left out though, because for the consumer it is the absolute worst time to be in town: Traffic grinds to a halt and the sales staff are checking out the show, doing their homework so they can better help you later on.

What about Hickory? It's best to avoid furniture shopping in the state altogether during this time. The salespeople from Hickory are running off to High Point to attend Market too, and there is an air of general pandemonium when it comes to shopping for furniture at these times of the year. The best way to avoid intersecting with Market is to call the High Point Chamber of Commerce or to check their Web site. Dates are set years in advance, so there's no worry of it sneaking up on you.

One good thing about Market is the *after-Market sales*. Stores begin selling off their market samples within weeks of the end of Market and it's a great time to capitalize on the savings. Other regular sale times include after-holiday markdowns. Many stores also offer warehouse-style clearance sales but the dates vary from one retailer to the next.

With the exception of Market (and a few weeks leading up to it) there is no bad time of year to make your trip to North Carolina. It's always good to check in with the Convention and Visitors Bureau before you finalize your plans. You may decide that you want to plan your visit to coincide with another seasonal event or attraction, like High Point's Shakespeare Festival (which is scheduled annually from August through October), or perhaps you'd rather avoid another like the Central Carolina Cat Fanciers Show (January) because it reminds you of Fluffy—who was left at home.

MINIGUIDES

INSIDER'S GUIDE TO CASE GOODS

The term "case goods" refers to most wooden furniture, such as chests of drawers. As opposed to "upholstered seating," the other half of the furniture world where there may be a wood frame but that frame is upholstered and invisible, in case goods the wood is visible and prominent—the finish is critically important. Chris and Thad Bergelin, third- and fourth-generation case goods manufacturers and co-owners of Robert Bergelin Co. in Morganton, North Carolina, suggest you look for the following features when trying to identify great case goods:

1. Dovetailed drawers front and back. Dovetailing is a method of joining two pieces of wood to make a corner. It involves carving trapezoid-shaped notches in one piece, and similarly shaped teeth in the other piece. It is an extremely strong and durable method of joining wood that, when done with care, can last for hundreds of years. The best drawers are joined this way. Pull out a drawer and examine all its joints. Do they look as though they'll stand the test of time? Drawers take a lot of abuse, so you'll want them to be sturdy.

2. Smooth drawer insides. Great furniture can in part be judged by the sanding and finishing work that has been done to the parts you don't actually see when standing in front of the piece. Run your hand around the inside of the drawer. Does it feel smooth to the touch? This is another mark of quality.

3. Wood drawer guides and drawers that don't stick. The best drawers glide on wooden tracks. Although metal mecha- nisms are easier to pro-  duce and install, they are more prone to damage. All-wood construction is an indication that the man- ufacturing process has been a thorough one.

4. Tight-fitting joints. A high-quality piece of case goods furniture should have solid, durable, tight- fitting joints at every place where two pieces of wood meet. Examine the joints, and give them a push. Pick up one corner to see how much flex is in a case. There should be very little looseness. All wood furniture will flex a little bit, but if there is too much, the piece will probably not stay together for the long haul.

 5. Attention to detail on all sides. Examine the entire piece of furniture, especially the back, bot- tom, and inside of the case. This is where sloppy work and shortcuts are likely to reveal themselves.

6. Doors should swing and latch without resistance. It is especially important to make certain that pieces with doors have levelers on the base to adjust to the floor variations. Otherwise, an uneven floor (and most floors are at least a little bit uneven) will interfere with the smooth operation of doors.

7. Don't be scared of veneer; just try to understand it. Both solid wood furniture and veneer furniture can be good quality. Veneer doesn't automatically indicate bad furniture and when used wisely, it can bring down the cost without sacrificing quality or appearance. However, veneer on particleboard or MDF is prone to sag, so on dresser tops and long pieces there should be a center support to reduce the sag.

8. Dining table slides should work smoothly and table leaves should fit well. Legs should be extremely stable—if the table wobbles now, imagine it after you've used it every day for a year or two.

INSIDER'S GUIDE TO UPHOLSTERED SEATING

You can't see the inside of a couch, but there are still ways to know you're getting quality (or not). Charlie Greene, a furniture manufacturer and owner of Classic Gallery Furniture in High Point, North Carolina, gives this advice to those shopping for quality upholstered seating:

1. Be as rough with the furniture on the showroom floor as you would be with it in your home. Grab it, squeeze on the arms, press down hard on the pillows. Lie on it, sit on it for a while, make sure it's right for you and is tough enough to stand up to what you're planning to dish out.

2. Take one corner, any corner of the sofa or seat, and lift it. Does anything else lift with it? On a quality piece, the whole frame should move together. On a lower quality piece, you can lift one leg and the other three will stay on the ground.

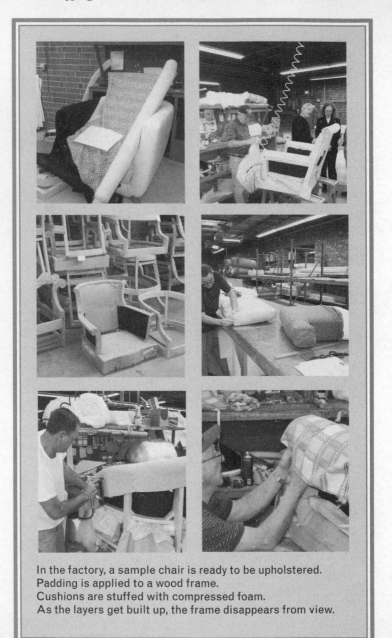

In the factory, a sample chair is ready to be upholstered.
Padding is applied to a wood frame.
Cushions are stuffed with compressed foam.
As the layers get built up, the frame disappears from view.

3. Don't let aesthetics distract you from the most important issue: Is it comfortable?

4. When sitting on the furniture, feel around carefully. There shouldn't be any surprises: You shouldn't feel any springs, boards, or elements of the frame. It should be as though the furniture is only the upholstery. If you're aware of the frame or the hardware, that's not good.

5. Can you get up out of it? You're going to sit and get up, sit and get up, many thousands of times once you purchase a piece of furniture, so make sure this process isn't going to be arduous or unpleasant for you. Think of your guests and older relatives as well.

6. Think of all seating as divided into two categories: furniture you sit "in" and furniture you sit "on." If you're planning to sit "in" a piece of furniture, you'll want it to have some give and plushness to it. But if you're going to sit "on" it, the whole thing should be quite firm.

7. Ask yourself what you'll be using the furniture for. Will it go in the den for relaxing, television viewing, and daily use? Or will it be in the formal living room for occasional use and more formal occasions? Different furniture serves different needs. There are so many factors that should be determined by use, yet people too often ignore the intended use of furniture when they buy it.

8. Are the cushions and pillows attached? Unattached cushions add life to the piece: You can fluff them and rotate them for longevity, and even replace them, just as you would with your car's tires.

INSIDER'S GUIDE TO LIGHTING

There's little point in taking the trouble to acquire beautiful furniture and accessories, and to create a beautiful home, if nobody is going to be able to see it. Lighting is the great misunderstood and often neglected aspect of home decorating. Carlos Butler, president and an owner of Butler's Electric Supply, gives these suggestions for lighting your home to make it look its best:

The selection doesn't end with furniture: Accessories, such as lighting, are well represented in North Carolina, too.

1. Furniture is the focus of a room. Your lighting and accessory choices will likely flow from the furniture. When choosing lighting fixtures, try to make them either complement the style of your furniture or at least not clash with it.

2. Quality lighting is an investment, just like quality furniture. Good lighting seems expensive, what with many chain and department stores offering $20 lamps that to the naked eye look a lot like their $200

brethren. But not only will good-quality lighting last longer, it will also provide better light and make everything in the room look better. Good lighting—and plenty of it—is also an investment in the health of your eyes.

3. The most important room in the house to light well is the kitchen. A poorly lit kitchen looks bad, and it's dangerous. Here it's recommended that a variety of light sources be combined to provide superb overall illumination: Overhead lighting for general illumination, task lighting to illuminate countertops without shadows, special lighting over the stove or other areas that demand extra light, and even recessed, cove, and kick-space lighting for decorative accent.

4. When purchasing a chandelier, it's absolutely essential that you have accurate measurements. In particular, you must know the height of the ceiling from which you plan to hang the chandelier to know if it will be appropriate for the room. Few people—even experts—can judge a chandelier's appropriateness for a given room without the benefit of measurements. It also helps to check with an electrician before you buy the chandelier to make sure you can get power up to the place on the ceiling where it's needed.

5. Outdoor lighting should be plentiful and powerful. They may look big enough in a showroom, but the great outdoors is a big place to illuminate. Again, accurate dimensions of your yards, patios, and walkways will be very helpful in making the selection.

6. When lighting a bathroom, be sure to measure the sizes of your vanities and accessories. Most lighting

will have to be worked around the locations of mirrors and other pre-installed elements. It's helpful to have a well-lit bathroom, because so much personal grooming takes place there and good lighting will help you to look your best.

7. Think about the purpose of lighting before choosing it. Do you lie on a certain couch in order to read? If so, a reading lamp is called for. Do you want to illuminate artwork hanging on a wall? If so, highly focused and directed lighting makes sense for that purpose. General illumination is often best provided indirectly, by light that doesn't glare or shine in people's eyes or create too many shadows. The more you think about what you want to light and how you want to light it, the better you'll be able to make the right lighting decisions.

8. There's no right or wrong in lighting, just as long as you get yourself enough light.

INSIDER'S GUIDE TO HOME DESIGN

From starter homes to mansions, when you set out to decorate a home it can be a daunting process. Sally Bently, owner and founder of Designing Women, established 1986 in Hickory, North Carolina, provides this advice to get you started:

1. What you buy should reflect your personal taste and sense of style, and the taste of the people who actually have to live in your home. It shouldn't reflect your mother's, brother's, sister's, or cousin's taste, or the taste of a magazine stylist who puts together pretty rooms that nobody lives in.

2. If a piece of furniture doesn't sing to you, don't even think about buying it. You're going to have to live with your furniture purchases for years—perhaps for the rest of your life. Don't get anything you don't absolutely love.

3. Complete one room at a time. Everyone is on a budget, whether it's $5,000 or $100,000. If you can't afford to furnish your whole house right away, move through it one room at a time, over a longer period of time. Don't try to buy one piece of furniture for every room, otherwise you'll be unhappy with every room. Be sure you complete the room you've started with the budget you have before you start buying furniture for others.

4. Shop for furniture with an open mind. You may find something you love that you didn't know existed—or that you never imagined you'd like.

5. Tear out pictures of things you like and put them in a file. Look at them after a week, a month, and two months. This is the best way to predict whether you'll love your furniture in the long term. You'll likely find that half of the pictures you selected are no longer appealing to you. You're evolving all the time and you want to be sure that your furniture can grow with you.

6. Make sure the people living in the room(s) in question are happy with the selections you've made. You don't want to buy a formal chair for the den where your husband wants a recliner. Furniture has to be purchased with people's needs in mind.

7. It's important to know the parameters of your home when making furniture decisions. For example, if you

have kids and dogs running around the house all the time, you'll want to be a bit more practical than if you're a retired couple with a low-impact lifestyle.

8. Try to have fun when choosing furniture, and see it as a rare opportunity to do something nice for yourself. You are furnishing your home, your nest, your inner sanctum.

9. Keep things in perspective: Let's face it, no one is going to die as a result of furniture shopping. In the end, it's just a couch, a bed, or a dining room table so be sure to keep it real and have fun.

10. Don't bring the church committee along with you. Too many cooks spoil the broth. If you must have *one* friend with you, let them walk around and meet up for a coffee break or lunch. But it's *your* home and you make the decision for yourself.

11. Don't cheat on upholstery. It's expensive, but it's the last thing you want to cut corners on.

12. Don't be scared to ask for help, or to hire a designer.

TOP 5 LISTS

Following is my compilation of Top 5 Lists wherein I indicate my preferences in each of several categories. It is important to note that these are my personal favorites. The lists are subjective and based on a number of different factors (overall quality, quality-to-price ratio, craftsmanship, customer service, and so forth), not just the final product that the manufacturer or store may provide.

TOP 5 LARGE RETAILERS

1. Rose (High Point, see p. 85)
2. Wood-Armfield (High Point, see p. 101)
3. Boyles (High Point main store, see p. 61, and also the group of Boyles galleries in the Hickory Furniture Mart, see p. 170)
4. Blacks (High Point, see p. 57)
5. Hickory Park (the group of Hickory Park galleries in the Hickory Furniture Mart, see p. 179)

TOP 5 SMALL RETAILERS

1. Utility Craft (High Point, see p. 95)
2. Robert Bergelin (High Point and Hickory, see p. 122)
3. Home Focus (Hickory Furniture Mart, see p. 182)
4. Studio 70 (Catawba Furniture Mall, Hickory, see p. 202)
5. High Point Furniture Sales (High Point, see p. 76)

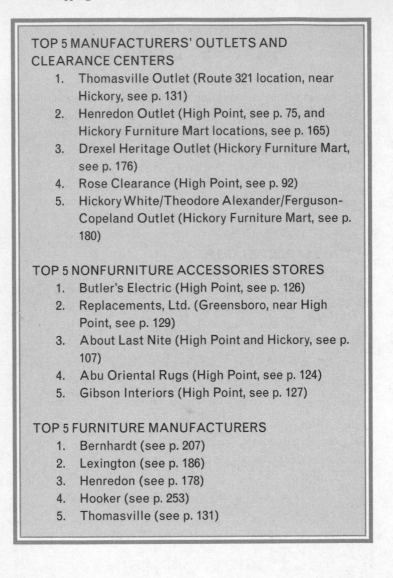

TOP 5 MANUFACTURERS' OUTLETS AND
CLEARANCE CENTERS

1. Thomasville Outlet (Route 321 location, near Hickory, see p. 131)
2. Henredon Outlet (High Point, see p. 75, and Hickory Furniture Mart locations, see p. 165)
3. Drexel Heritage Outlet (Hickory Furniture Mart, see p. 176)
4. Rose Clearance (High Point, see p. 92)
5. Hickory White/Theodore Alexander/Ferguson-Copeland Outlet (Hickory Furniture Mart, see p. 180)

TOP 5 NONFURNITURE ACCESSORIES STORES

1. Butler's Electric (High Point, see p. 126)
2. Replacements, Ltd. (Greensboro, near High Point, see p. 129)
3. About Last Nite (High Point and Hickory, see p. 107)
4. Abu Oriental Rugs (High Point, see p. 124)
5. Gibson Interiors (High Point, see p. 127)

TOP 5 FURNITURE MANUFACTURERS

1. Bernhardt (see p. 207)
2. Lexington (see p. 186)
3. Henredon (see p. 178)
4. Hooker (see p. 253)
5. Thomasville (see p. 131)

High Point
(Including Thomasville)

When you pull into High Point for the first time, you might be tempted to say, *"This* is the Home Furnishings Capital of the World???" Downtown High Point doesn't necessarily make a great first impression. But the more time I've spent in High Point, and the more I've peeled away its layers, the more I've grown to appreciate it.

For one thing, the folks in High Point are some of the nicest people you'll find anywhere on Planet Earth. For another thing, if you look a little closer at the Downtown area, you'll notice that there is some truly gorgeous modern architecture all around you. Moreover, though there's not a whole lot to do by big city standards, there's more than enough to keep a curious person occupied for a week or more. There's even some great local food, and of course there's all that furniture shopping.

Aside from the Atrium Furniture Mall and a few of the smaller specialty stores, all the major High Point furniture shopping is out on the highways and byways away from Downtown. But don't skip Downtown altogether. It's where you'll find the Convention and Visitors Bureau—a critical first stop on any visit, with an outgoing and superinformed staff—as well as the area's best hotels and restaurants, the Furniture Discovery Center, and even the inimitable World's Largest Chest of Drawers.

This chapter begins with some basic information about High Point. Then, the bulk of the chapter is a listing of the major furniture retailers, outlets, and clearance centers in the High Point area (as well as in nearby Thomasville). Finally, the chapter includes key information about lodging, dining, and attractions in and near High Point.

STORE LISTINGS

⇥ = top pick

American Accents Clearance Center
1300 S. Main Street
(336) 885-1304
Hours: 9:00 AM–6:00 PM Monday–Friday, 9:00 AM–
    5:30 PM Saturday; closed Sunday and major holidays

Ashley Interiors
310 S. Elm Street
(336) 889-7573
(336) 889-7574 (fax)
www.ashleyinteriors.com
Hours: 9:00 AM–5:00 PM Monday–Saturday; closed Sun-
    day, major holidays, and during Market (April and
    October)

Authorized dealer for Braxton Culler
Annual sales: March and September
Established: 1986 (Braxton Culler 1975)
Size: 30,000 square feet
Number of sales staff: three (two with formal design education)
Telephone sales are accepted
Shipping available nationwide with recommended carriers
Payment policy: 35 percent down as deposit, balance due when ready to ship; Visa and MasterCard accepted
Store manager: Jill Bowen

The specialty of the house is the Braxton Culler line of wicker and rattan furniture for bedroom, living and dining rooms, and total outdoor-proof sets, but you'll find a full selection of quality upholstered furniture, too. The Braxton Culler line dates to 1975 and was founded by R. Braxton Culler III. The company manufactures both wicker/rattan and upholstered furniture in a casual, colorful, diverse, and relaxed style.

Braxton Culler, based in High Point, has grown from 35,000 square feet of manufacturing space in 1975 to more than 250,000 square feet today. The company started with upholstered furniture, and began manufacturing its very successful wicker and rattan collections in 1982. The product lines also include occasional tables, étagères, dining groups, and armoires.

►► Black's Furniture
2800 Westchester Drive (Highway 68)
(336) 886-5011
(336) 886-4734 (fax)
E-mail: *blacks@highpoint.net*
www.blacksfurniture.com
Hours: 9:00 AM–6:00 PM Monday–Friday,

9:00 AM–5:00 PM Saturday, closed Sunday, January 1,
Thanksgiving, Christmas
Authorized dealer for more than 200 manufacturers,
including:

American Drew
American of Martinsville
Art de Mexico
Artistica
As You Like It Lamps
Baldwin Brass Beds
Barcalounger
Bassett
Bassett Mirror Company
   (BMC)
Benicia Foundry Beds
Berkline
Bevan Funnell
Bradington Young
Braxton Culler
Brown Jordan
Bucks County Collection
C.R. Laine
Cal-Style
Carlton McLendon
Carsons
Casa Bique
Century
Chapman
Charleston Forge
Chatham County
Christian Mosson
Chromecraft
Classic Gallery
Classic Leather

Classic Rattan
Clayton Marcus
Cochrane Casegoods
Colgate Baby Mattress
Cooper Classics
Corsican Brass Company
Cox
Craftique
Craftwork Guild
Crawford
Creative Metal
Crystal Clear
CTH—Carolina Tables
Daystrom
Decorative Arts
Decorative Crafts
Denny Lamps
Elliotts Designs
Emerson Et Cie
Emerson Leather
Entrée
Fairfield Chair
Fashion Bed Group
Ficks Reed
Fine Arts Lamps
Flexsteel
Frederick Cooper
Friedman Mirrors
Garcia Imports
George Kovacs

Glass Arts

Globier

Grace Mfg.

Grandeur Beds

Great City Traders

Guildmaster

Hammary

Hart Industries

Hekman

Henry Link Wicker

Hickory Hill

Hickory Leather

Hickory-White

High Point Furniture

Hood

Hooker

Howard Miller

Hyundai

Impressions by Thomasville

International Carolina
  Glass

International Images by
  Salterini

Jasper

Johnston Casuals

Kingsdown Bedding

La-Z-Boy

Lam Lee Group

Lane

Lane "A La Carte"

Leathercraft

Lee

Library Lamps

Link Taylor

Lloyd Flanders

Lyon Shaw

Madison Square

Marbro Lamps

Mario

McKay Table Pads

McKinley Leather

Meadowcraft

Mikhail Darafeev

Moosehead

Nathan Hale

Nora Fenton

Null

Ohio Table Pads

Old Hickory Tannery

OLF Oriental Lacquer

Passport

Pearson

Pennsylvania Classics

Peters Revington

Plant Plant

Pulaski

Quotizel

Rex Furniture

Riverside

Rowe

Sam Moore

Sarried

Sedgefield

Sedgewick Rattan

Serta Mattress

Shady Lady

Sherrill Occasional

Sligh

Southern Reproductions

Stakmore

Stanton Cooper   *Uwharrie Chair*
Statesville Chair   *Vanguard*
Stiffel Lamps   *Vaughan*
Superior Furniture   *Vaughan Bassett*
Swaim   *Victorian Classics*
Swan Brass Beds   *Virginia Metalcrafters*
Taylor Woodcraft   *Weiman*
Telescope   *Wesley Allen*
Thayer Coggin   *Westwood Lamps*
Traditional Heirlooms   *Wexford*
Tropitone   *Wildwood*
Tyndale Lamps   *Winston*
Universal   *Woodard*
Uttermost   *Woodmark*

Annual sales: February and August
Established: 1964
Size: 45,000
Number of sales staff: nine (eight with formal design education)
Telephone orders accepted as per individual manufacturer guidelines
Nationwide delivery
Payment policy: one-third down as deposit, remainder due upon delivery in certified check or money order
Store Manager: Wanda Cox

Black's is a mid-sized store with a friendly and welcoming staff. It is owned by a former employee and her husband and there is a comfortable, cozy, and personable feel to the business. Employee seminars including "integrity-based selling" are a requisite part of the ongoing sales training at Black's. Translation services are available for Greek, Spanish, German, Italian, and Arabic. Black's offers a true all-in-one home-décor shopping experience with the addition to its onsite shop called Dramatic Draperies, where it's possible to purchase bed treatments (duvets, coverlets, spreads), window treatments (blinds, draperies, custom features), as well as a wide variety of special-order fabric.

> *"Down here, furniture is a way of life. It's in our blood: I knew what eight-way hand-tied meant when I was ten years old."* CHRISTINA RHEIN, SALESPERSON, BLACK'S

⤛ **Boyles Furniture**
5700 Riverdale Drive (at Business 85 and Riverdale Drive)
Jamestown
(336) 812-2200
www.boyles.com
Hours: 8:30 AM–5:30 PM Monday, Tuesday, Wednesday, and Saturday; 8:30 AM–8:30 PM Thursday and Friday; closed Sunday and major holidays
Authorized dealer for well over 100 manufacturers including:

Ambience Lighting
American Drew
Artex Table Pads
Baker
Benicia Foundry
Bernhardt
Bevan Funnell
Bradington Young
Cape Craftsman
Carvers Guild
Casa Stradivari
Century
Chapman Lamps

Charleston-Forge
Chelsea House
Councill Craftsman
Cox
C.T.H. Sherrill
Decorative Crafts
Designmaster
Drexel Heritage
Entrée
Fine Art Lamps
Frederick Cooper
Fremarc Designs
Friedman Brothers

Garcia Imports

George Kovacs

Gloster

Great City Traders

Guildmaster

Guy Chaddock

Habersham Plantation

Hancock & Moore

Harden

Hart

Hekman

Henkel-Harris

Henredon

Hentschel Clocks

Hickory Chair

Hickory White

Hooker

Howard Miller

Hunt Country

Ital Art Design

Jeffco

Jessica Charles

John Richard

Karges

Kenroy

Kincaid

Kindel

Kinder Harris

Kingsdown

La Barge

Lane

Lane Venture

Lexington

Lillian August

Madison Square

Maitland-Smith

Majestic Mirror

Marbro Lamps

Marge Carson

Milling Road

Motioncraft

Natural Light, The

Nichols & Stone

Old Granite Tannery

Pennsylvania House

Platt

Precedent

Pulaski

Quoizel Lighting

Ralph Lauren

Replogle Globes

Riverside

Robert Abbey

Royal Patina

Sam Moore

Sarreid LTD

Sealy

Sedgefield

Sherrill

Southampton

Southern

Southwood

Stanley

Tapestries LTD

Taylor King

Theodore Alexander

Thomasville

Timberwood Trading

Urban Classics

Virgina Metalcrafters

Waterford Lighting   Wildwood Lamps
Wellington Hall   Winston
Wesley Allen   Woodard
Whitmore Sherrill   Wright Table Company
Wildwood Accents   Ziba Rug Gallery

Annual sale: June
Established: 1949
Size: 85,000 square feet
Number of sales staff: 39 (six with formal design education)
Telephone/Internet sales accepted as per individual man-
    ufacturer restrictions
Nationwide delivery
Payment policy: One-third down as deposit, balance (if
    not previously paid in full) due upon delivery; at time
    of purchase cash, checks, certified funds, MasterCard,
    and Visa are accepted; *upon delivery certified funds only*.
Store manager: Anthony Lockhart

There are 12 Boyles stores in North Carolina and this one
is the flagship. Though all of the stores are beautifully
appointed and full of highly experienced sales staff, this one is
meant to be the crown jewel of the empire. Expect to see
medium- to high-end manufacturers' lines arranged tastefully
in mixed showrooms simulating an in-home feel, as well as
galleries dedicated to showcasing individual manufacturers.
You'll find it all here: dining rooms to dens, cottage to formal
furnishings. And you can complete each look with accessories,
too. And it all arrives to your home under the professional
watch and care of Classic Moving & Storage, exclusive to
Boyles and specializing in white-glove service (literally).

Not to be overlooked too, for those who cannot or do not
wish to travel, Boyles now has a handful of dedicated sales
staff working solely on Internet sales. You can develop a working relationship with one of these salespeople and, working

within and abiding by the various manufacturer restrictions, you can furnish a room or an entire home without ever having to leave your easy chair.

Nearby, also see Boyles at: 616 Greensboro Road, (336) 884-8088.

In Hickory, see Chapter 3, Hickory Furniture Mart listings.

Buy-Rite Furniture, Inc.
2619 S. Main Street
(336) 886-1206
(336) 886-1208 (fax)
Hours: 9:00 AM–6:00 PM Monday–Saturday, 12:00 PM–
6:00 PM Sunday.
Specializes in market samples, closeouts, and showroom
samples
Annual sales: Tent sale in April and October in addition
to clearance center
Established: 1995
Size: 52,000 square feet
Number of salespeople: five (one with formal design ed-
ucation)
Telephone/Internet orders are accepted
Nationwide delivery
Payment policy: Payment in full at time of purchase
Store Manager: Rebecca Moore

It's all about one-of-a-kind opportunities at Buy-Rite because the specialty of the house is market samples, closeouts, and showroom samples. That means that available selections are on the floor and are sold as-is.

Capa Imports
319 N. Main Street
(336) 885-9999
(336) 885-2850 (fax)

Hours: 9:00 AM–5:00 PM Tuesday–Saturday; closed Sunday, Monday, and major holidays
Nationwide delivery
Payment policy: Payment in full at time of purchase; cash, check, Visa, and MasterCard accepted

Capa is not just an importer of rugs from Turkey, India, Pakistan, China, and Iran but is also the manufacturer, so you can expect factory direct prices and Capa encourages you to compare. Other products include case goods from Indonesia and a wide selection of accessories from China.

Central Furniture Outlet, Inc.
2352 English Road
(336) 882-9511
(336) 882-0212 (fax)
Hours: 9:00 AM–5:30 PM Tuesday–Saturday; closed Sunday, Monday, and major holidays
Size: 16,000 square feet
Nationwide delivery
Payment policy: Payment in full at time of purchase; cash, check, Visa, MasterCard, and Discover accepted

A true clearance center, Central sells market and photography samples of nationally recognized manufacturer brands directly off the showroom floor. Selections, though variable, often include dining room, living room (including leather), and bedroom furnishings as well as kitchen furniture, rugs, and accessories.

Furnitureland South
5635 Riverdale Drive
(336) 841-4328
(336) 841-1397 (fax)
www.furniturelandsouth.com

Hours: 8:30 AM–5:30 PM Monday, Tuesday, Wednesday, and Saturday, 8:30 AM–8:30 PM Thursday and Friday; closed Sunday and major holidays
Authorized dealer for 400 manufacturers including:

A.A. Laun
Acacia Furniture, Inc.
Action Industries, Inc.
All Continental
Allusions
Ambiance Imports, Inc.
Ambience Lighting &
    Accessories
American Bedding Ind.,
    Inc.
American Drew
American Impressions, Inc.
American Mirror
    Company
American of Martinsville
Andrew Pearson Design
Anichini
Ann Gish
Antiques & Interiors
Antler Art, Inc.
Aquarius Mirrorworks
Arbek Furniture Mfg.,
    Inc.
Ardley Hall
Art Image
Art Up
Artagraphic Reproduction
Artisan House, Inc.
Artisans

Artisans Design Guild
Artistica Metal Designs,
    Inc.
Artmax, Inc.
As You Like It, Inc.
Ashley Manor, Inc.
Aspen Furniture
Athol Table Mfg.
    Company, Inc.
Atlanta Glasscrafters
Aubergine Home
    Collection
Austin Sculpture's, Inc.
Avantglide
Azzolin Bros.
Baldwin Hardware
    Corporation
Banana Fish
Barcalounger Company
Bassett Mirror Company,
    Inc.
Basta Sole By Tropitone
Bauer Lamps
Bean Station Furniture
    Factory
Bellino Fine Linens
Benchcraft, Inc.
Benicia Foundry & Iron
    Works

Berco Tableworks, Ltd.
Berkline Corporation
Bernhardt Furniture
  Company
Bestar
Bevan Funnell Ltd.
Bibi Continental
  Corporation
Big Fish, Inc.
Blacksmith Shop, Inc.
Bodrum Group, The
Bontempi
Boussac Fadini, Inc.
Bradington Young
Braxton Culler, Inc.
Broyhill Furniture
  Industries, Inc.
Bush Industries (Eric
  Morgan)
Butler Specialty Company
Cal-Bear, Inc.
Cambridge Lamps
Cape Craftsmen, Inc.
Carey Moore Designs
Carolina Mirror Company
Carson's of High Point
Carvers Guild
Casa Bique, Ltd.
Casa Stradivari
Casey Collection
Cast Classics Landgrave
Casual Lamps
Casual Living Worldwide
Cebu Imports, Inc.

Century Furniture
Cfi Manufacturing, Inc.
Chapman Manufacturing
  Company
Charles Alan International
Child Craft Industries, Inc.
Christy USA, Llc.
Chromcraft Corporation
CJC, Inc.
Clark Casual
Classic Gallery, Inc.
Classic Leather
Classic Rattan, Inc.
Clayton Marcus Company,
  Inc.
Cochrane Furniture
  Company, Inc.
Coja Leatherline of
  Canada, Inc.
Collections '85, Inc.
Collezione Europa
Colonial Furniture
  Company
Columbine Cody
Comfortaire Corporation
Conover Chair Company,
  Inc.
Corsican Company
Cox Manufacturing
  Company, Inc.
Craft-Tex, Inc.
Craftique, Llc.
Craftwork Guild, Ltd.
Creations At Dallas

Creative Decor
Creative Fine Arts, Inc.
Creative Ideas
Cresswell Lighting
Crystal Clear Industries
Currey & Company, Inc.
Cwl Designs
D & F Wicker Rattan
 Imports
Dale Tiffany, Inc.
Dalyn Rug Company
Daystrom Furniture, Inc.
Dayva International
Decorative Crafts
Deitz & Sons, Inc.
Design Guild
Design Source, Ltd.
Design South Furniture
Design Systems South, Inc.
Designs By Robert
 Guenther
Deszign, Inc.
Dillon Furniture
Dimplex North America
Dinaire, Llc.
Directional
Distinction Leather
Distinctive Designs
 International
Dmi Custom Bedspreads
Drexel Heritage
 Furnishings
Dura Hold
Duralee Fabrics, Ltd.
Dutailier Group, Inc.

Eastern Accents
Eckadams/Vogel Peterson
 Company
Elements By Grapevine,
 Inc.
Elliotts Designs, Inc.
Ello International
Englander Sleep Products
Espino
Euroreps, Inc.
Evan Du Four, Inc.
Evans Ceramics/California
Excelsior Designs, Inc.
Expressive Designs
Fabric to Frame, Inc.
Fabrica International
Fairfield Chair Company
Fashion Bed Group
Ficks Reed Company
Fine Art Lamps
Flair Design
Flexsteel Industries, Inc.
Florita-Nova, Inc.
Focus Rugs
Forma & Design, Inc.
Frederick Cooper Lamps
 Company, Inc.
Fremarc Designs
French Heritage
 Reproductions
Friedman Bros.
Fusion Z
Galtech Corporation
Georgian Furnishing
 Company, Ltd.

Gianni
Gloster Furniture, Inc.
Grace Mfg.
Great City Traders
Guildmaster, Inc.
Gunlocke Company, The
H. Potter
H.K.H. International
Hamilton Collections, Inc.
Hammary
Harris Furniture
  Reproductions
Harris Lamps/Jaru
Hart Associates
Hedge Row Decorative
  Outdoors
Heirloom Furniture
Hekman Furniture
Henry Link
Hickory House Furniture
  Company
Hickory Springs Mfg.
Hickory White Company
High Point Billiard
  Designs
High Point Furniture
  Industries
Highland House of
  Hickory, Inc.
Historic Golf Prints
Hollywoods, Inc.
Howard Miller Clock
  Company
Hubbardton Forge
Humane Trophies

Huntington House
  Furniture
Huppe
Hydra Designs, Inc.
Hyundai Furniture
  Industries
Idea Industries, Inc.
Ideal Originals
Import Collection, The
Inmon Enterprises, Inc.
Interactive Health
Jackson of Danville
  Originals
James R. Cooper, Ltd.
Jamestown Manor
Jasper Cabinet Company
Jaynor Furnishings
Jd Store Equipment
Jdi Group
Jensen Jarrah Leisure
John Boos & Company
John Richard Collection
Johnston Benchworks
Johnston Casuals
Jon Elliott Company
Jsf Industries
Jsp-Les Industries
K. Highsmith, Inc.
Kaiser-Kuhn Lighting,
  Ltd.
Karastan
Katha Diddel Home
  Collection
Keller Furniture
Kenroy International

Kessler
Kessler Collections
Key City Furniture
  Company
Kinder-Harris, Inc.
King Hickory Furniture
  Company
Kingsley-Bate
Koch & Lowy, Inc.
Koch Originals
Koko Company, Inc., The
Kravet Fabrics, Inc.
La Barge, Inc.
Lady Slipper Design
Ladybug
Lambs & Ivy
Lane Company, Inc.
Lane Venture Excursions
  Living
Latex Foam Products, Llc.
Laurier Furniture, Ltd.
Le Blanc Linen Wash
Lea Industries
Leathercraft
Leathertrend
Leeazanne Lamps
Leedo Furniture
Legacy (By Friendly
  Hearts)
Legacy By Child Craft
Leggett & Platt, Inc.
Leisters Furniture, Inc.
Leisure House, Inc.
Lenox Lighting (China)
Lexington Home Brands

Limonta Home
Lloyd/Flanders Industries,
  Inc.
Lodi Down & Feather
Lorraine
Lotus Arts, Inc.
Lucia Cassa Textiles
Lux-Art Silks, Inc.
Lyon-Shaw, Inc.
M.T.S. Besana-Carrara
Madison Square
  Furniture, Inc.
Magnussen/Presidential
Maharam
Maitland-Smith U.S., Inc.
Mallin Corporation
Marbro
Marcella Fine Rugs
Marlow Furniture
  Company, Inc.
Marvel Group, Inc.
Masland Carpets, Inc.
Mastercraft Imports, Ltd.
Masterlooms
Masterpiece Accessories
Meadowcraft
Metropolitan Galleries
Mikhail Darafeev, Inc.
Millender Furniture
  Company
Miller Desk
Minoff Lamps
Mirror Craft
Mohawk Furniture
  Company, Inc.

Momeni, Inc.
Montage Moon
Movi, Inc.
MTS Seating
Murobello
Murray Feiss Import
    Company
Mystic Valley Traders, Inc.
N.C. Souther
Natural Light, The
Natuzzi
Nautica Home
Nichols & Stone Company
Nini Ferrucci Designs, Inc.
Norman Perry Lamps
North Bay Collections
Null Industries, Inc.
Ofs
Ohio Table Pad Company
Oklahoma Importing
    Company
Old Hickory Furniture
    Company
Oldcastle Specialty
Olf, Inc.
Orbit Design, Inc.
Oriental Weavers, Sphinx
    Div.
Original Plant Plant, The
P & P Chair Company
Pacific Coast Lighting
Palecek Imports, Inc.
Paper White
Paragon Pictures
Park Place Corporation

Parker Southern
Pastiche
Pavilion
Payne Street Imports
Peacock Alley
Pearson
Pennsylvania House
    Furniture
Pentaura Limited
Piage & Pieta Art Stone
Pieri Creations
Pine Creek Bedding
    Company
Portobello International
Powell Company, The
Premier Bedding Group
Preview Furniture
    Corporation
Privilege House, Inc.
Pulaski Furniture
    Corporation
Quoizel, Inc.
Raffia
Reliance Lamp Company,
    Inc.
Rembrandt Lamps
Remington Lamp
    Company
Ren-Wil, Inc.
Renoir Designs
Reprocrafters
Reverie Dreamy Linens
Rex Furniture Company,
    Inc.
Ridgeway Clocks, Inc.

Ridgewood Furniture, Inc.
Riverside Furniture
Robert Abbey, Inc.
Robert Allen Fabrics, Inc.
Rug Barn, The
Sagefield Leather
Salem Square
Saloom Furniture
  Company, Inc.
Sam Moore Division, Inc.
Samsonite Furniture/
  Sunlite Casual
San Miguel Trading
  Company
Sandicast
Sarreid, Ltd.
Savoir Faire Decor
Savoy House
Scangift, Ltd.
Schnadig Corporation
Schweiger Division of
  KCS, Inc.
Sea Gull Lighting
Sealy Furniture of
  Maryland
Second Avenue Design
Second Impressions
Sedgefield By Adams
Serta Mattress Company
Sferra Bros., Ltd.
Shadow Catchers
Shashi Cann
Shaw Industries, Inc.
Shelby Williams
  Industries, Inc.

Sheres
Shuford Furniture
Sidney Arthur, Inc.
Sierrarts, Ltd.
Signature Designer Rugs
Silk-Like By Labs
Silver Furniture
  Company, Inc.
Simmons Bedding
  Company
South Cone Trading
  Company
Southport Furniture, Inc.
Sovereign, Ltd.
Spring Air Mattress
  Corporation
St. Timothy Classics
Stakmore
Stanley Furniture
Statesville Chair Company
Statton Furniture Imports
Statton Furniture Mfg.
  Company
Stein World, Inc.
Steven Drew International
Stevenson & Vestal
Stiffel Lamps
Stock Market, The
Stone County Ironworks
Stone International
Stoneleigh
Stratford Company
Strobel Technologies
Stroheim & Romann, Inc.
Style Upholstering, Inc.

Stylex
Summer Classics
Sumter Cabinet Company
Sunlite Casual Furniture,
   Inc.
Sustainable Lifestyles, Llc.
Swaim Classics
Swaim Occasional
Swedish Blonde Corporation
Table Designs
Telescope Casual
   Furniture, Inc.
Temple, Inc.
Tempur-Pedic, Inc.
Textillery
Thayer Coggin, Inc.
Thief River Linen
Three Coins Import, Ltd.
Timmerman Mfg.
Touchstone Fine Art
Toyo Trading Company
Tradition House, Inc.
Tree Factory, Inc.
Triad Butcher Block
Triune Business Furniture
Tropitone Furniture
   Company, Inc.
Trowbridge Gallery
Tucker Design, Ltd.
Two Day Designs
Two's Company, Inc.
Tyndall Creek Furniture
   Company
Tyne House of Lewes,
   England

Ultegra Office Furniture
Union City Mirror &
   Table Company
Unique Lamp Creations
Unique Originals, Inc.
Universal Furniture
   Industries, Inc.
Urban Woods
Uttermost Company, The
Uwharrie Chair Company
Valspar
Van Teal
Vanguard Furniture
   Company
Vantage Industries, Inc.
Vaughan Furniture
   Company, Inc.
Vaughan-Bassett
   Furniture Company
Veneman Collection
Venture By Lane
Versteel
Victorian Classics
Virginia Metalcrafters
Vitafoam Incorporated
   Feather Beds
Vitalie Mfg. Company
Vogel Peterson
Wade Furniture
Wara Intercontinental
   Company
Watson Furniture
   Systems
Webb Furniture
Weiman Company

Wellington Hall Caribbean
   Corporation
Wellington Hall, Ltd.
Wesley Allen, Inc.
Westwood Lighting Group,
   Inc.
Whitecraft Rattan, Inc.
Whoa!
Wildcat Territory

Wildwood Lamp
   Company
Willow Creek Collection
Windsor Collections
Windsor Home Collection
Winners Only, Inc.
Woodard Company, The
Woodland Furniture, Llc.
Woodmark Originals

Established: 1969
Size: Over 1,000,000 square feet
Number of sales staff: 183
Telephone orders are accepted
National and international delivery available
Payment policy: Cash or personal check upon order,
   balance in cash or certified funds upon delivery

   Furnitureland South is by far the largest of all of the furniture stores in High Point. If you can't find the style, or an approximation thereof here, you'll likely not find it anywhere (though notably the store does not carry Thomasville). You've got to admire the determined and brilliant businesspeople behind this operation: They have grown and grown and made their entire reputation by word of mouth without any real advertising. But biggest doesn't necessarily mean best and sometimes size can even be a detriment. For some customers, having too many choices of similar items can be overwhelming. As is the case at all of the stores, finding the right salesperson to work with is critical, and because of the sheer volume and size of this behemoth, finding the right salesperson to help you is all the more important. My own personal customer-service experiences shopping incognito at Furnitureland South have not been fantastic, but the store has many, many dedicated fans.

Giorgio Home Furnishings

125 S. Hamilton Road (directly behind the Radisson
  Hotel, two blocks)
(336) 883-1991
(336) 883-1906 (fax)
Hours: 10:00 AM–"through the cocktail hour" Tuesday–Saturday (if you want more specifics, call for details and see if *you* can nail them down); closed
  Sunday, Monday, and major holidays
Nationwide delivery
Payment policy: 50 percent down as deposit, balance due
  prior to shipping

Manufacturer direct, Giorgio is a designer and manufacturer of contemporary furniture for home and office. A full-
service operation, the staff at Giorgio works with you to
choose the best furnishings for your environment even if that
includes "writing the specs for the entire décor." One of a kind.

⤙ Henredon Factory Outlet

641 W. Ward Avenue
(336) 888-2844
www.henredon.com
Directions: West off the 1100 block of S. Main Street
  near downtown
Hours: 10:00 AM–5:00 PM Monday–Friday, 10:00 AM–
  3:00 PM Saturday; closed Sunday and major holidays
Exclusive Henredon outlet
Sales: Periodic promotions throughout the year, variable
  timing
Established: 2000
Size: 30,000 square feet
Number of sales staff: three (one with formal design
  training)

> *"If you can find the husband his easy chair first thing, he'll be a lot happier shopping along the rest of the way."* —MAUREEN MALLON, DIRECTOR OF MARKETING, FURNITURELAND SOUTH

No telephone sales

Delivery: Shipping can be arranged but pick-up of purchases is encouraged

Payment: Payment in full upon purchase

Henredon is among the finest furniture manufacturers, with a legendary international reputation. Were money no object, we'd all surely have a lot of Henredon furniture in our homes. Located adjacent to the Henredon High Point showroom for Market, this store sells samples, and discontinued and "slightly distressed" items. Should you be so lucky as to find what you're looking for, you'll likely strike it big with savings. Be sure to check items carefully because all purchases are as-is and final. No custom orders.

✦ High Point Furniture Sales

200 Baker Road

(800) 834-1875

(336) 841-5664

(336) 885-7034 (fax)

www.highpointfurnsales.com

Hours: 8:30 AM–5:30 PM Monday–Friday, 9:00 AM–4:30 PM Saturday, closed Sunday and major holidays

Authorized dealer for approximately 200 major manufacturers including:

American Drew	*Artistic Impressions*
American Mirror	*Austin Art*
Andrew Pearson	*Balangier*
Arnold Palmer	*Baldwin Brass*

Baldwin Clocks

Barcalounger

Barn Door

Bauer Lamps

Benicia Beds

Berkshire

Bob Timberlake

Bradington Young

Brass Craft, Inc.

Braxton Culler

Brown Jordon

Broyhill

Cambridge Lamps

Cape Craftsman

Carlton Mclendon

Carolina Mirror

Carson S

Carter Furniture

Casabique

Cebu

Charisma Chairs

Charter Table Company

Chatham County

Chromcraft

Clark Casual

Classic Rattan

Clayton Marcus

Cochrane Furniture

Conover Chair

Cox Mfg.

Crawford Mfg.

Creations At Dallas (Hill)

Crystal Clear Industries

Dar Ran

Darafeau

Decorative Crafts

Design Masters

Dillon

Dinaire

Distinctive Designs

Dutailier

Ello

Excelsior

Fabricoate

Fairfield Chair

Fashion Bed

Murray Feiss

Ficks Reed

Fine Arts Lamps

Fitz & Floyd

Flexsteel

Floral Arts

Fredrick Cooper

Friedman Brothers

Friendship Uph.

Glass Arts

Grace

Great American Trading
    Company

Great City Traders

Greene Bros.

Guildmaster

Halcyon

Hammary

Henry Link

Hickory Hill

High Point Furniture
    Industries

Hollywoods

Hooker

Howard Miller Clock
Huntington House
Hyundai
International
Jasper Cabinet
Jeffco
Johnston Casuals
Keller
Key City
Kimball
Kincaid
Kinder Harris
Kingsdown
Lane
Laurier
Lea
Leisters
Lexington Furniture
Link Taylor
Lloyd Flanders
Lyon-Shaw
Marlow
Mary Dale Lamp
Master Design
Miller Desk
Mirror Craft
Mobel
Murray Feiss
Natural Light
Null Mfg.
Oriental Lacquer
Ohio Table Pad Company
Palecek
Paragon
Park Place

Patrician
Peoplelounger
Peter Revington
Phillips Furniture
Pier
Pinnacle
Plant Plant
Preview
Pulaski
Regency House
Remington Lamps
Rex Furniture
Richardson Bros.
Ridgeway
Riverside
Rowe Furniture
Rug Barn
Sam Moore
Samsonite
San Diego Design
Santee
Schnadig
Schweiger
Sealy Mattress
Sedgefield Lamps
Serta Mattress
Shafer Seating
Sherill Occasional
Signature Rugs
Skill Craft
Stanley
Stiffel Lamp
Stratalounger
Stratford
Swaim Originals

Taylorsville Uph.

Telescope

Thayer Coggin

Thomasville Furniture

Timeless Bedding

Toyo

Tropitone

Universal Mfg.

Us Furniture Industries

Uttermost Mirrors

Uwharrie Chair

Van Patten

Van Teal, Inc.

Vanguard

Vaughan-Bassett

Vaughan Furniture

Venture

Victorian Classics

Weiman

Wesley Allen

Winston

Woodard

Woodmark

Established: 1983

Size: 25,000 square feet

Number of sales staff: seven (two with formal design education)

Telephone/Internet orders accepted in accordance with manufacturer's stipulation

Payment policy: 25 percent deposit by cash, check, and credit card (Visa and MasterCard)

Balance on delivery by certified check or money order

Store owners: Earline Richardson, Larry Cecil

High Point Furniture Sales is a bit off the beaten track but it's worth the trip. The staff is friendly and the co-owners are right out there on the floor working to help customers along with the rest of the sales staff. The selection is extensive and there is a nice eclectic collection of practical and playful furniture catering to varying budgets—not just high end.

La Barge Outlet
411 Tomlinson Street
(336) 812-2420
(336) 887-2625

Hours: 9:00 AM–5:00 PM Monday–Saturday; closed Sunday, major holidays and during Market (in April and October)

Exclusive La Barge outlet

Sales: Periodic promotions throughout the year, variable timing

Established: 1982

Size: 12,000 square feet

Number of sales staff: five (two with formal design education)

Telephone sales are accepted for items that are on the floor—all sales are final—no returns

Delivery: Shipping can be arranged but pick up of purchases is encouraged

Payment: Payment in full upon purchase; cash, check, and all major credit cards are accepted

Store manager: Lesa Pierce

La Barge specializes in Continental European–style furnishings including chairs, occasional tables, and mirrors. What you see is what you get—it's all samples and discontinued and "slightly distressed" items, many of which are one of a kind. Should you be so lucky as to find what you're looking for, you'll likely strike it big with savings. Be sure to check items carefully because all purchases are "as is" and final. No custom orders.

Lincoln-Gerrard USA, Inc.
1949 West Green Drive
(336) 889-9555
(336) 889-9559
www.lincolngerardusa.com
Hours: 10:00 AM–5:00 PM Monday–Saturday, closed Sunday and major holidays

Dealer for Lincoln Gerard/St. Martin's Lane; this store
represents the manufacturer
Established: This store was established in 1991, the man-
ufacturer was established in 1978
Size: 50,000 square feet
Number of sales staff: four (one with formal design
training)
Telephone/Internet orders are accepted
Store manager: Maureen P. Griffith M.S.I.D.A.

The collection of 18th-century mahogany antique replicas
at Lincoln-Gerrard is highly regarded and from the moment
you enter the store it isn't difficult to see why. The pieces here
are more akin to art—it's the type of furniture that gets
handed down from one generation to the next.

⤛ **Maitland-Smith Outlet**
411 Tomlinson Street
(336) 812-2420
(336) 887-2625
www.maitland-smith.com
Hours: 9:00 AM–5:00 PM Monday–Saturday; closed Sun-
day, major holidays, and during Market (April and
October)
Exclusive Maitland-Smith outlet
Sales: Periodic promotions throughout the year, variable
timing
Established: 1982
Size: 12,000 square feet
Number of sales staff: five (two with formal design edu-
cation)
No telephone sales
Delivery: Shipping can be arranged but pick-up of pur-
chases is encouraged
Payment: Payment in full upon purchase

Maitland-Smith is a manufacturer (and designer) of 17th-
and 18th-century English-style furniture. Dining room
tables, china cabinets, desks, game tables, and even entertainment centers (to name a few) are constructed with elaborate
wood veneers. Mirrors, hanging art, curio cabinets, lighting,
and chandeliers are also part of the selection. Here you will
find Market samples and discontinued and "slightly distressed" items, many of which are one of a kind. Should you
be so lucky as to find what you're looking for, you'll likely save
big. Be sure to check items carefully because all purchases are
"as is" and final. No custom orders.

National Home Furnishings Center (Kagan's)
1628 S. Main Street (corner of Market Center Drive)
Hours: 9:00 AM–6:00 PM Monday–Saturday
Size: 80,000+ square feet
Nationwide delivery
A mini furniture mall featuring three independent stores,
  Kagan's National Home Furnishings Center includes:

1. *Kagan's Furniture Galleries*
   (336) 883-7113
   (336) 883-7177 (fax)

2. *Decorator's Choice*
   (336) 889-9058
   Authorized dealer for Dinec, Trica, Vermont Precision,
     Morlow, Morgan Stewart
   Annual sales: Dates are variable
   Established: 1990
   Size: 7,000 square feet
   Number of sales staff: two
   Telephone orders accepted
   Nationwide delivery

Payment policy: Visa, MasterCard, and personal checks
accepted; all orders must be paid in full before shipping

With a wide selection of transitional and contemporary furniture, Decorator's Choice has a friendly staff dedicated to
helping you find the right furniture to suit your personal look.
Also visit Decorator's Choice in the Atrium Furniture Mall.

3. *Gibson Interiors* (see Special Nonfurniture Store Listings for
description)
   (800) 247-5460
   (336) 883-4444

Pennsylvania House Furniture Outlet
1300 N. Main Street
(336) 887-3000
(336) 887-0329
www.acollectorsgallery.com
Authorized dealer for:

American Drew	Hammary
Barcalounger	Hekman
Cox	Howard Miller
Craftique	Lea Children
Crawford	Parker Southern
Emerson Et Cie	Pennsylvania Classics
Fauld Town & Country	Pennsylvania House
Flexsteel	Serta
Grace Metal	Statesville Chair
Green Bros.	

Annual sales: January and August
Established 1996
Size: 15,000 square feet
Number of staff: four

Telephone/Internet orders accepted
Nationwide delivery
Payment policy: 50 percent down as deposit, balance due
    before shipping; cash, check, Visa, MasterCard, and
    Discover accepted
Store manager: Betsy Callahan

Pennsylvania House has been making furniture since 1892, and the company wouldn't still be in business if the product hadn't been satisfying generations of customers. The selection here includes North Carolina's largest gallery of Pennsylvania House furniture plus lots of other favorite manufacturers. The store is an authorized Pennsylvania House factory outlet, but here the same rules don't apply: You can buy anything off the floor at outlet store prices—market samples, factory closeouts, and scratch-and-dent—but you can *also* custom order any item at the regular price.

Also visit Pennsylvania House in the Atrium Furniture Mall.

Reflections Furniture
(336) 885-5180
(336) 885-5188 (fax)
www.reflectionsfurniture.com
Hours: 9:00 AM–6:00 PM Monday–Friday, 9:00 AM–
    5:00 PM Saturday; closed Sunday and major holidays
Authorized dealer for:

American Leather	*John Charles Designs*
Axi	*Lazar*
Ekornes	*Natuzzi*
Elite	*Shermag*
Elite Tables	*Stone International*
Ello	*Trica*
Gamma	*Visu*

Annual sales: February, May, July, and November
Telephone/Internet sales accepted as per manufacturer
  restrictions
In-home delivery/installation available
Payment policy: 50 percent down as deposit, balance due
  before shipping; MasterCard, Visa, Discover, cash,
  and personal checks accepted

A family owned business, the specialty here is leather. The emphasis is on contemporary furnishings and unique accessories but there is also a selection of transitional and traditional furnishings (upholstery, tables, lamps, rugs, entertainment, dining) to round out the mix. One of three stores that this Belgian immigrant family owns, they started with a mere 1,000 feet and have grown to 20,000 in total. Custom orders available.

See also stores in the Hickory Furniture Mart (listed in Chapter 3) and Charlotte: 11235 Carolina Place Pkwy., Charlotte, NC 28134 (Pineville), (704) 341-6262, (704) 341-9828 (fax).

⤙ **Rose Furniture Company**
916 Finch Avenue
(336) 886-6050
(336) 886-5055 (fax)
www.rosefurniture.com

"We're like a little chamber of commerce here—we keep maps, give restaurant suggestions, and tell people where to stay. Don't be afraid to ask us about anything—not just furniture. You'll get a real Southern experience when you walk through our door."
—SUE KURTZ, OUTLET MANAGER FOR MAITLAND-SMITH, LA BARGE, HENREDON

Hours: 8:30 AM–5:00 PM Monday–Friday, 8:30 AM–
4:00 PM Saturday; closed Sunday, January 1, July 4,
Thanksgiving, December 25 & 26
Authorized dealer for over 600 manufacturers including:

A.A. Laun
Aberdeen Furniture
Acacia Furniture
Accent Fine Art Collection
Accessories International
Action Industries
Albert M. Lock Company
Alexandra Diez
American Drew
American Furniture
Craftsmen
American of High Point
American Mirror
Company
American Rug Company
Amish Country Collection
Andrew Pearson
Anne David Thomas
Anthony of California
Ap Industries
Ardley Hall
Arlington House
Armstrong Furniture
Company
A.R.T.
Art Gallery
Arte De Mexico
Artisan House
Artistica Metal Designs
As You Like It

Ashley Furniture
Industries
Ashley Manor
Austin Sculpture
Ayers/Chairmakers
Baldwin Clocks
Baldwin Dinettes
Baldwin Hardware
Company
Banks Coldstone
Barclay-Rowe Accessories
Barn Door
Barlow Tyrie
Barton Reproductions
Bashian Rugs
Bassett Mirror Company
Bauer International
Beach Mfg.
Beechbrook
Benchcraft
Benicia Bed
Bentwood Furniture, Inc.
Berkline
Berkshire
Bermex
Bernhardt
Best Chairs
Best Imports, Inc.
Beth Weissman
Bevan Funnel, Ltd.

Blacksmith Shop

Boyd Furniture Company

Bradington Young

Brady Furniture Company

Braxton Culler

Bristol House

Brown Jordan

Broyhill

Builtright Chair Company

Burris Industries

Butler Specialty Company

C.R. Laine

Cambridge Lamps

Canal Dover

Candella Lighting

Capel Rugs

Carlton Mclendon

Carolina Mirror Company

Carsons

Carter Contemporary

Carver's Guild

Casa Bique

Casa Stradivari

Casey Collection, The

Casual Lamps

Century Furniture
   Company

Chapman

Charleston Forge

Charter Table Company

Chelsea House

Chromcraft

Clark Casual

Classic Leather

Classic Rattan

Clayton Marcus

Cochrane Furniture

Corona Decor Company

Corsican/Swan Brass Bed

Councill Business
   Furniture

Councill Craftsmen, Inc.

Craftmark
   Convertibles/Occasional

Craftwork Guild

Crawford

Creative Metal & Wood

Crystal Clear Galleries

Crystal Clear Lighting

Cth-Sherrill Occasional

D. & F. Wicker Rattan
   Imports

D.M.I. Furniture
   Company

Dale Tiffany, Inc.

Dar/Ran

Davis & Davis

Dawson Furniture
   Company

Daystrom Furniture

Decorative Crafts, Inc.

Denunzio, H.A. Company

Design Guild

Design Horizons

Dfc

Dillon Furniture

Dinaire Corporation

Directional

Distinction Leather

Douglas Furniture

Dresher
D.R. Kincaid
D-Scan—The Danwood
   Collection
Dummy Book Company,
   The
Dutailier
Eco Wood
Elements By Grapevine
Elliott's Designs
Ello
Emerson Et Cie
Emerson Leather
Eric Morgan
Erwin Lambeth
Excelsior Designs
Executive Leather
Exotic Furniture
Fairfield Chair Company
Faith Walk Designs
Fashion Bed Group
Ficks Reed Company
Fine Art Lamps
Flat Rock
Frederick Cooper
Fremarc Designs
Friedman Bros./Decorative
   Arts
Friendship Upholstery
Froelich Furniture
   Company, The
Game Room
Garcia Imports
George Kovacs
Georgian Furnishings

Glass Arts by Icg
Gloster
Grosfillex
Guardsman Products
Guildmaster
H. & H. Furniture
H.T.B.
Habersham Plantation
Hale of Vermont
Hammary Furniture
   Company
Hammock Source
Harris Lamps
Hart Associates
Hekman Furniture
   Company
Hen-Feathers & Company
Heritage Haus Furniture
Heyward House-Heygill
   Imports
Hickory Chair
Hickory Hill
Hickory Tavern
Hickory White
High Point Desk
Hitchcock Chair
Hollywoods
Homecrest
Hooker Furniture
Howard Miller
Idi
International/Karpen
Iron Classics
Italmond
J. Royale

J.S.F. Industries

Joal–James Langley

Johnston Casuals

John Widdicomb

Kaiser Kuhn Lighting

Karges

Kings Creek

Kingsdown Mattress
    Company

Kingsley-Bate

Koch & Lowy

Kushwood Mfg.

C.R. Laine

Lane Action

Lane Company

Lane Venture

Lea Industries

Leathercraft

Leatherman's Guild

Leatherworks

Leggett & Platt

Leisters Furniture

Lenox

Lloyd Buxton

Lloyd/Flanders

Lorts

Lyon Shaw

Madison Square

Marbro Lamp

Massoud Furniture
    Company

Master Design Furniture

McKay Custom Table Pads

McKinley Leather

Miami Metal

Michael Thomas
    Furniture

Millenium

Minoff Lamp

Mirror Fair

Moderno

Mohawk Finishing
    Products

Moosehead Furniture
    Company

Motioncraft

Murray Feiss Industries

Nathan Hale

National of Mt. Airy

Natural Light

New England Clock
    Company

Nichols & Stone

Norman Perry

Null Industries

Old Hickory Tannery

Palecek

Paoli

Pawley's Island Hammock

Pennsylvania Classics

Pennsylvania House

Peters-Revington

Philip Reinisch

Pilliod

Plant Plant

Platt

Pompeii

Powell Company

Powell—"Lifechest"

Precedent

Preview Furniture
  Company
Proptronics
Pulaski
Quoizel
Ridgeway Clocks
Riverside Furniture
Robert Allen Fabrics
Robinson
Roxton Temple Stuart
Royal Patina
Royce Corporation
St. Timothy
Salem Square
Sam Moore Chairs
Samsonite Furniture
  Company
Samuel Lawrence
Sarreid, Ltd.
Schnadig Corporation
Schweiger
Sealy Bedding &
  Mattresses
Sealy of Maryland
Sedgefield By Adams
S.E.E. Imports
Singer
Southern of Conover
Southwood
Spring Air
Stakmore Company
Stanford Upholstery
Stanley
Statesville Chair
Statton

Stein World
Stiffel Lamps
Stone International
Style Upholstery
Swaim
Taylorsville Upholstering
Telescope
Temple Stuart
Temple Upholstery
Thayer Coggin
Thomasville
Tianjin-Philadelphia
Tropitone
Tyndale
Universal Furniture
  Company
Uttermost Company
Uwharrie Chair
Vanguard Furniture
  Company
Vaughan-Bassett
Vaughan Furniture
  Company
Venture
Victoria Furniture
Villageois
Virginia House Furniture
Virginia Metalcrafters
Waterford Crystal
Waterford Furniture
  Makers
Waverly
Webb Furniture
Wellington Hall
Wesley Allen

Whitaker Furniture
  Company
Whitecraft Rattan
Wildwood Lamps &
  Accessories
William Allen, Inc.

Winners Only
Woodard
Woodmark
Yorkshire Leather, Ltd.
Young-Hinkle

Established: 1925
Size: 180,000 square feet
Number of sales people: 85
Telephone/Internet orders accepted as per individual
  manufacturer guidelines
Nationwide delivery
Payment policy: One-third down as deposit with personal check, balance due upon delivery in certified
  funds; if you are on a tight delivery schedule you can
  expedite your order by sending a copy of your check
  to Rose in advance—this will save you the time it
  takes for the bank to clear your check, which for out-
  of-state checks can be a week or more
Store manager: Todd Kester

As an overall great shopping experience, Rose is my clear
favorite of all the High Point big boys. Not only is it the oldest furniture store of its kind in High Point, but it is also into
its fourth generation of family employees, the selection is as
extensive as at any competitor, and the sales staff couldn't be
nicer, more helpful, or more professional. Obviously, with 85
salespeople, they aren't all family members—but they might
as well be.

The overwhelming attitude is that the salespeople are
happy to be there, they're happy you—the consumer—is
there, they have decades of collective sales experience under
their belts, and they really want to help you find what you
need. These are not people who are going to try to sell you a

sectional when what you need is a chair, just to make a commission. These are serious career salespeople who want you to leave their store happy (and that's how they think of it, as *their* store), regardless of whether they sell you a lamp or a houseful of furniture. Reputation and word of mouth are the best advertisements and they know it. Some of these salespeople will sheepishly admit they initially sold to one generation and these satisfied customers referred not only friends but, over the years, also referred their children and grandchildren. You don't hear about that kind of customer satisfaction very often. Though I am confident that all of the sales staff at Rose is more than competent, well informed, and pleasant to work with, my personal favorite is Tim Shepard.

> Also visit:
> Rose on Main—"Your Furniture Value Center"
> 1813 S. Main Street
> (336) 878-5010
> 25,000 square feet

Catering to a starting price point, Rose on Main attracts a lot of younger Generation-X types, though that's not an exclusive statement. Rose on Main fills a niche for people in every phase of life looking to spend a little less on furniture. All tastes and styles—from traditional to transitional and even contemporary—are on display and there is also an extensive outdoor furniture selection from manufacturers like Winston and Tropitone.

and

> Rose Furniture Clearance
> 2020 Logan Street (across the street from Rose Furniture)
> (336) 878-5030

Expect to see closeouts, scratch-and-dents, and discontinued items in a warehouse-type setting, at great reductions.

Sklar-Peppler Showroom

210 Main Street (one-half block south of the Radisson
    Hotel)
(336) 882-7586
(336) 882-7585 (fax)
www.sklarpeppler.com
Hours: 9:00 AM–4:30 PM Monday–Friday, 9:00 AM–
    1:30 PM Saturday; closed Sunday, major holidays, and
    throughout the months of April and October
Authorized dealer for Sklar-Peppler
Nationwide delivery
Payment policy: 50 percent down as deposit, balance due
    upon delivery, payable by cash and certified funds

A leading upholstery manufacturer in Canada since 1945, Sklar-Peppler offers a complete line of traditional, transitional, and contemporary products: sofas, chairs, loveseats, and sleeper beds. Dozens of fabrics are available to personalize your furniture for custom orders. Don't miss the outlet section where special sales on showroom samples are discounted to make room for incoming new designs.

Stickley

225 N. Elm Street
(336) 887-1336
(336) 887-5214 (fax)
www.stickley.com
Hours: 9:30 AM–5:30 PM Monday–Saturday; closed Sunday, holidays, and during Market
Exclusive North Carolina authorized dealer for Stickley
Established: 2001 (see below for more detail)
Size: 25,000 square feet

Number of sales staff: four (all with formal education in interior design)

Delivery: Stickley has authorized dealers around the country and all orders are placed through the dealer closest to the customer; delivery is available through the authorized dealers

Store manager: Sally McGrogan

The Stickley brand was established in 1900 and sits at or near the pinnacle of the furniture industry. Even if you've never heard the name Stickley, you will recognize the distinctive Mission-style furniture with its vivid vertical lines. This retail store, a revolution for the Stickley company, was established in 2001. Previously, this showroom was open only during Market and only to industry people. There are no special

The unmistakable look of Stickley's Mission-style furniture.

discounts available at this store that wouldn't be available at your regional authorized dealer, however the High Point store has the distinction of displaying the *entire* line of Stickley furniture and latest fabrics, something no other dealer can afford to do. By no means would I suggest making a special trip to High Point to visit Stickley but if you are coming to shop and you're interested in the brand, this is the best place to see it.

➤ **Utility Craft**
2630 Eastchester Drive
(336) 454-6153
(336) 454-5065 (fax)
www.utilitycraft.com
Hours: 9:00 AM–5:30 PM Monday–Friday, 9:00 AM–
    5:00 PM Saturday; closed Sunday and national holidays
Authorized dealer for over 300 major manufacturers in-
    cluding:

Allusions	*British Traditions*
Ambience	*Broyhill*
American Drew	*California House*
Andrew Pearson	*California Kids*
A.P. Generations	*Cambridge*
Ardley Hall	*Camden*
Artistica	*Canadel*
Arttra	*Cape Craftsman*
As You Like it, Inc.	*Capel*
Avant-Glide	*Carsons*
Big Fish	*Carver's Guild*
Bob Timberlake	*Casa Bique*
Botanica	*C.B.S. Imports*
Bradington Young	*Century*
Braxton Culler	*Chair Works*

Chapman
Charleston Forge
Chromecraft
Clark Casual
Classic Leather
Classic Rattan
Clayton Marcus
Cochrane
Colonial Furniture
Comfort Designs
Cooper Classics
Corsican
Councill
Cox
C.R. Laine
Craftwork Guild
Crawford
Creative Elegance
Cresent
C.T.H. Sherrill
Currey & Co.
Custom Craft
Dauphine Mirror
Davis Cabinet
Designmaster
Destinations by Century
Dillon
Elegant Earth, The
Elem. by Grapevine
Elliots
Ello
English Imports
Entree
Excelsior

Exotic Furniture
Fairfield Chair
Fashion Bed
Ficks Reed
Fine Art Lamps
Fine Art, Ltd.
Flat Rock
Florita-Nova, Inc.
Fortune Rattan
Frederick Cooper
Fremarc
Friedman Bros.
Garcia Imports
Grace
Great City Traders
Guildmaster
Habersham
Hammary
Harper
Hart
Hekman
Henry Link
Hickory Chair
Hickory–White
Hilda Flack
Hollywoods
Hooker
Howard Miller
H.T.B./Lane
Hurtado
Jasper Cabinet
J.D.I.
Jenigere
John Richards

Johnston Casuals
J. Royale
J.S.F.
Kimball
Kinder Harris
Koch
Labarge
Lane
La-Z-Boy
Lea
Lexington
Lloyd Flanders
Lyon Shaw
Madison Square
Maitland Smith
McKay Table Pad
Michael Thomas
Mikhail Darafeev
Miles Talbott
Millennium
Montaage
Moosehead
Motioncraft
Nichols & Stone
Nora Fenton
Ohio Table Pad
Our House Designs
One of a Kind
Palacek
Parker–Southern
Parlance
Paul Robinson
Pavilion
Pentura, Ltd.

Phillip Reinisch
Phillips Collection
Phoenix Art
Pompeii
Prestige Arts
Rex
Richardson Bros.
Riverside
Robert Abbey
Robin Bruce
Royal Patina
Salem Square
Sam Moore
Sarreid
Schnadig Corporation
Sealy
Sedgefield
Serta
Shadow Catchers
Shuford
Soicher Marin
South Cone
Southampton
Southwood
Stanford Upholstery
Stanley Furniture
Statesville Chair
Statton
Stoneville
Superior
Swaim
Tapestries, Ltd.
Textillery
Thayer Coggin

Theodore & Alexander
Timberwood
Tomlin Designs
Tyndall, Inc.
Universal
Uttermost Company, The
Vanguard
Veneman
Venture
Vitale
Waterford

Waterford Crystal
  Lighting
Wellington Hall
Wesley Allen
Wesley Hall
Wildwood
Winston
Woodard
Woodmark
Yorkshire House

Annual sales: February and August
Established: 1949
Size: 12,000 square feet
Number of sales staff: six (two with formal design education)
Telephone/Internet orders accepted per individual manufacturer guidelines
Nationwide delivery
Payment Policy: One-third down as deposit, payable by cash, check, money order, and major credit cards; balance payable upon delivery by cash, cashier's check, or money order
Store manager: Sue Snipes

"If you're working on furnishing an entire house, make an appointment with a salesperson in advance so they can block out a couple of days from their schedule and work with you completely uninterrupted." —TODD KESTER, MANAGER AND FOURTH-GENERATION ROSE FURNITURE FAMILY

Utility Craft provides one of High Point's most intimate and comfortable furniture shopping experiences. It's a small store by the standards of the region, but don't let that fool you: Utility Craft packs a whole lot of furniture into a limited amount of space, and through catalogs you can pretty much order anything at Utility Craft that you could order at one of the larger places. The store offers competitive prices, extensive accessories, full service, and, perhaps most importantly, an exceptional sales staff.

I particularly like the personal touches like the customer locator map (customers "pin" their hometowns on a map), the wall of thank-you letters to salespeople, and the wall of history detailing the background of the store's original owners. The first-generation owners made furniture by hand, and perhaps that's why the store carries so many small independent lines. The owners, the Kennetts, also own Wood-Armfield downtown.

> *"We spend as much time with a customer as they need, whether they're buying a candle or a sleeper or furnishing an entire home."*—SUE SNIPES, MANAGER, UTILITY CRAFT

Wagner's Furniture Outlet

2001 Brentwood Street (off Business 85 at Brentwood exit)

(336) 884-7253

Hours: 9:00 AM–6:00 PM Monday–Friday, 9:00 AM–5:00 PM Saturday; closed Sunday and major holidays

Nationwide delivery

Payment policy: Payment in full at time of purchase

Expect to see Market samples, factory closeouts, overstocks, "duplications," and clearance items from retail stores on recognizable national manufacturers. As with all of the outlets the same rules apply: Big savings if you luck into a piece you like, but all purchases are final and products are "as is."

Warehouse Discount Furniture

2515 S. Main Street (one-half mile south of Business
   I-85)
(336) 885-6200
(336) 885-6242 (fax)
www.warehousediscountfurniture.com
Hours: 9:00 AM–6:00 PM Monday–Friday, 9:00 AM–
   5:00 PM Saturday; closed Sunday, December 24 & 25,
   January 1
Authorized dealer for:

Bermex	*Liberty*
Friendship	*Simmons*
Hickory Mark	*Vaughn Bassett*
Katnapper	

Annual sales: May, October/November
Established 1999
Size: 20,000 square feet
Number of sales staff: eight (two with formal design edu-
   cation)
Telephone/Internet orders are accepted
Nationwide delivery
Payment policy: 50 percent down as deposit; balance due
   prior to delivery; orders totaling less than $800 re-
   quire payment in full; cash, certified check, and major
   credit cards are accepted
Store manager: Mike Boggs

Market samples as well as first quality in solid mahogany, cherry, and oak bedroom and dining room suites are available. Also available are leather, upholstery, and special orders.

Whitewood Industries
215 S. Main Street
(336) 885-5706
(336) 885-9830 (fax)
www.whitewood.net
Hours: 9:30 AM–4:30 PM Monday–Friday, 10:00 AM–
   2:00 PM Saturday; closed Sunday, major holidays, and
   throughout the months of April and October
Established: Company since 1982
Nationwide delivery
Payment policy: 50 percent down as deposit, balance in
   certified funds due upon delivery; cash and check
   accepted

Imported case goods in all kinds of designs and finishes are
available in factory samples, closeouts, and warehouse inventory. Selection includes tables, chairs, kitchen and dining
rooms, stools, rockers, hutches, and buffets.

↠ **Wood-Armfield**
460 S. Main Street
(336) 889-6522
(336) 889-6505
www.woodarmfield.com
Hours: 9:00 AM–6:00 PM Monday–Friday, 9:00 AM–
   5:00 PM Saturday; closed Sunday and major holidays
Authorized dealer for dozens of manufacturers including:

Allusions	*Arttra*
Ambience	*As You Like It, Inc.*
American Drew	*Avant-Glide*
Andrew Pearson	*Bernhardt*
Ardley Hall	*Big Fish Botanica*
Art Image	*Bob Timberlake*
Artistica	*Bradington Young*

Braxton Culler
British Traditions
Broyhill
California House
California Kids
Cambridge
Camden
Canadel
Cape Craftsman
Capel
Carsons
Carver's Guild
C.B.S. Imports
Century
Chapman
Charleston Forge
Chromecraft
Clark Casual
Classic Leather
Classic Rattan
Clayton Marcus
Cochrane
Collections '85, Inc.
Colonial Furniture
Comfort Designs
Cooper Classics
Corsican
Councill
Cox
C.R. Laine
Craftwork Guild
Crawford
Creative Elegance
Cresent
C.T.H. Sherrill

Currey & Co.
Custom Craft
Dauphine Mirror
Davis Cabinet
Designmaster
Destination by Century
Elegant Earth, The
Exotic Furniture
Fine Art Lamps
Florita-Nova, Inc.
Fortune Rattan
Frederick Cooper
Fremarc
Friedman Bros.
Garcia Imports
Grace
Great City Traders
Guildmaster
Habersham
Hammary
Harper
Hart
Hekman
Henry Link
Hickory Chair
Hickory–White
Hilda Flack
Hollywoods
Hooker
Howard Miller
H.T.B./Lane
Hurtado
Ital-Art
Jasper Cabinet
J.D.I.

Jenigere

John Richards

Johnston Casuals

J. Royale

J.S.F.

Kimball

Kinder Harris

Koch

La Barge

Lane

La-Z-Boy

Lea

Lexington

Lloyd Flanders

Lyon Shaw

Madison Square

Maitland Smith

Mat Home

McKay Table Pad

Michael Thomas

Mikhail Darafeev

Miles Talbot

Millennium

Montage

Moosehead

Motion Craft

Natuzzi

Nichols & Stone

Ohio Table Pad

Our House Designs

Paul Robinson

Phoenix

Prestige Arts

Richardson Bros.

Riverside

Robert Abbey

Rowe

Royal Patina

Salem Square

Sam Moore

Sarreid

S. Bent

Schnadig Corporation

Sealy

Sedgefield

Serta

Shadow Catchers

Shuford

Soicher Marin

South Cone

Southampton

Southwood

Stanford Upholstery

Stanley Furniture

Statesville Chair

Statton

Stoneville

Superior

Swaim

Tapestries, Ltd.

Textillery

Thayer Coggin

Theodore & Alexander

Thomasville

Timberwood

Tomlin Designs

Tyndall Creek

Universal

Uttermost Company, The

Vanguard

Veneman	*Wesley Hall*
Venture	*Wildwood*
Vitale	*Winston*
Waterford	*Woodard*
Wellington Hall	*Woodmark*
Wesley Allen	*Yorkshire House*

Annual sales: February, May, August, September; also
   floor clearance items throughout the year
Established: 1939
Size: 160,000 square feet
Number of sales staff: 50
Telephone orders are variable based upon individual
   manufacturer restrictions; call for further information
National and international delivery
Payment policy: One-third down as deposit; balance and
   shipping due upon delivery; credit cards, cash, and
   check for deposit; balance payable in certified check,
   cash, or money order
Store manager: Kay Patseavouras

One of the top 100 furniture retailers in the country, it
comes as no surprise that Wood-Armfield, a family owned
business, has deep roots in the furniture industry. One of the
"mid-sized" (though massive by any other standard) High
Point furniture stores, Wood-Armfield incorporates the best

---

*"Customers select furniture based on emotion. It's not like
you're buying a set of tires—you want furniture that is going to
be comfortable and make you feel good."* —WANDA COX, CO-
OWNER OF BLACK'S FURNITURE AND VETERAN SALESWOMAN

of both worlds: It's big enough to have dozens of manufacturer's products displayed in a beautiful home-style setup, but it's not so large that you get lost in the store—or lost in the shuffle (as with some of the giants).

The sales staff is well trained, friendly, and up-to-date on the latest and greatest in furniture. Many have been in the furniture business for 20 years or more. There is a 5,000-square-foot design center where, with the help of your salesperson, you can work out room layouts, fabric selections, and other details of your furnishing needs. There is a Kids' Room where children can play or watch a video while parents are shopping. Owned by the same people who own the much smaller sister store Utility Craft, it's easy to see how the two are related— excellent and friendly sales staff and great selection—and why they rank so high on my favorites list.

NOTE: Wood-Armfield is connected to the Atrium furniture mall, and you can go from one to the other without ever having to go outside. Jessica's Café in the Atrium is a good spot for lunch or a break. You'll see many local businesspeople there in kind.

THE ATRIUM FURNITURE MALL

430 S. Main Street

(336) 882-5599

(336) 882-6950 (fax)

www.atriumfurniture.com

www.shopandstay.com

info@atriumfurniture.com

Hours: 9:00 AM–6:00 PM Monday–Friday, 9:00 AM–5:00 PM Saturday; closed Sunday and holidays: January 1, July 4, Thanksgiving, Christmas Eve and Day; also closed in the event of snow—call if there's any question

Almost 700 different manufacturers are represented amongst the different stores

Shipping: Individual stores arrange shipping and stores will work together to consolidate and ship orders if a customer buys from more than one store within the mall; the mall crew will pack and wrap customer carry-outs and help customers load trucks if they are taking their furniture with them

Established: 1988

Size: 225,000 square feet

Number of stores: 23 plus the Atrium Café upstairs and the café and refreshment area on the ground level

Mall contact information: General Manager: Jim Wall; Marketing Director: Judie Holcomb-Pack

Annual clearance sales: February: Mid-winter clearance sale; May: Spring after-Market sale; July: Summer clearance sale; November: Fall after-Market sale; there are other sales but dates are variable from store to store and from one year to the next

The Atrium Furniture Mall is one of two furniture malls in North Carolina owned by the Ikerd family. The mall concept has been a great success in High Point because people like the one-stop-shopping concept and the mall offers a relaxed, manageable atmosphere. It's a good solution for people who want to visit the "big boys" in High Point but also like the idea of shopping in a mall. This way you can do both all in the same town, and with Wood-Armfield (attached) next door you never have to go outside if, for example, it's snowing.

In addition to the Web sites listed under the individual store listings, each store in the Atrium has Web pages (including pictures of current stock and styles) on the Atrium's Web site.

Rest stop: On the first floor of the Atrium Mall (in the back) there is a peaceful sitting area, complete with tables, a soda fountain, popcorn machine, and a few other little treats—*all complimentary*—for shoppers to enjoy while they plan, regroup, and refuel for shopping the mall.

If you need something a bit more hearty, visit the Atrium Café [serving lunch 11:00 AM–4:00 PM Monday–Saturday; tel: (336) 889-9934] on the 3rd floor. You'll find not just shoppers patronizing the café but local business-people as well. It's a quick and easy solution, and all the more appealing when considering the extremely limited in-town dining options. All the food is cooked fresh and made-to-order on the premises.

About Last Nite (1st floor)
    (336) 885-9737
    (336) 885-1098 (fax)
    Hours: In addition to hours and holidays posted
        above, also closed New Year's Eve

Authorized linens dealer for: SDH-The Purist,
 Sferra, Peacock Alley, J. Clayton International,
 Bella Notte, Fleur de Lis, Home Treasures,
 Legacy, Matteo, Christian Aubry, Austin Horn,
 Fino Lino, Koko, Christy, Wildcat, Paper White,
 Sweet Dreams, Eastern Acents, Mystic Valley
 Traders, Lucia, Designs, Banana Fish
Also carry furniture manufacturers: Stone County,
 Old Biscayne Designs, Excavo, Stylecraft of
 Thomasville
Annual sales: January white sale, after-Market sale
 in May, after-Market sale in late October/early
 November.
Established: 2001
Size: 2,000 square feet
Number of sales staff: four (one with formal design
 education)
Nationwide delivery in the continental U.S., also
 combine to ship with other retailers in the area
Telephone/Internet sales are accepted
Payment policy: 50 percent due on deposit, remainder
 due at shipping; all major credit cards are ac-
 cepted
Store Manager: Allison Albright

Though not a furniture retailer, About Last Nite carries a wide selection of linens so fine, let's just say
they're good enough for the White House and the Vatican.
Thread counts range from 200 to 1,020. You'll want to go
around the store "rubbing and touching" as the friendly
sales staff is fond of saying. There is also a larger branch
of About Last Nite in the Catawba Furniture Mall in
Hickory.

Adams Furniture (1ˢᵗ floor)
  (336) 889-8090 (phone and fax)
  E-mail: *adamsfurn@aol.com*
  www.adamsfurniture.com
  Authorized dealer for Adams furniture
  Annual sales: Variable
  Established: At Atrium since January 2002
  Size: 3,650 square feet
  Number of sales staff: two
  Telephone orders accepted
  Nationwide delivery
  Payment policy: Payment in full for items purchased
     off the floor; orders from England require 50 per-
     cent down, balance due before shipping; cash,
     check, MasterCard, Visa, and American Express
     are accepted
  Store manager: Max Salsbury

The selection at Adams includes English antiques, authentic reproductions, traditional, and country furniture. Stock often includes one-of-a-kind pieces and floor samples (a very good lesson in illustrating how different styles and woods can successfully be mixed). Custom orders are available. Expect to wait 12–18 weeks for your masterpiece.

American Accents (3ʳᵈ floor)
  (336) 885-7412
  (336) 884-4171
  E-mail: *americanaccentsfurniture.com*
  Hours: 8:00 AM–6:00 PM Monday–Friday, 8:00 AM–5:00
     PM Saturday; closed: same as mall

Authorized dealer for a host of manufacturers including Bradco, Brown Street, Kingsley Bates, Dale Tiffany Lamps, Penns Creek, Royal Craftsman

Annual sales: March, September; 50-percent-off sale on most manufacturers

Established: 1983

Size: 17,000 square feet

Number of sales staff: six (four with formal interior design training)

Telephone orders accepted

Nationwide delivery

Payment policy: One-third down as deposit; cash and checks accepted

Store manager: Mike Shillinglaw

The largest selection in High Point of Shaker, Country, and Mission furniture and reproductions. Specializing in solid wood furniture, the majority of which is still being made by hand in the U.S.A.

Also visit:

American Accents Clearance Center
1300 S. Main Street
(336) 885-1304

American Reproductions (2nd floor, 2 stores)
(336) 889-8305
(336) 889-6166 (fax)
E-mail: *american@northstate.net*
www.americanreproductions.com

Authorized dealer for Lloyd Buxton, Taylor King,
  Oakwood Interiors Wisconsin, Tom Seely, De-
  signmaster, Sligh, C.R. Laine, Spring Air,
  Woodard, Fairfield, Braxton Culler, Winners
  Only, Corsican, Sam Moore, Blackhawk, River-
  side, Bassett, Designer Wicker, Legacy Classic,
  Brentwood, Waterford, Pulaski, Cox, Action
  Lane, Alexvale
Annual sales: Sales year-round
Established: 1989 (company established 1972)
Size: 36,000 square feet
Number of sales staff: seven (two with formal design
  training)
Telephone/Internet orders accepted
Nationwide delivery; consolidation of orders with
  other Atrium stores
Payment policy: 50 percent down as deposit in cash
  and check; up to $500 on a Visa, MasterCard, or
  Discover card over the phone; if you live in a
  COD state, the balance of the order and freight
  can be paid at time of delivery by certified funds;
  if you live in a non-COD state, the balance is due
  by personal check prior to delivery—call for details.
Store manager: Mark Hinkle

American Reproductions is a family owned and operated company established in 1972. With three stores in
North Carolina and one in High Point, American Reproductions is able to carry an extensive selection of manufacturers (450 between the different stores) and still
maintain a small store atmosphere.

Blowing Rock Furniture (4th floor)
(336) 885-2059
(336) 885-2068 (fax)
E-mail: *furnitureinfo@blowingrockfurniture.com*
www.blowingrockfurniture.com
Authorized dealer for:

A Touch of Elegance	Bruce Furniture
Academy Arts	Cape Craftsman
Alexander Julian	Capital Outdoor
All Continental	Carson's
American Atelier	Catnapper
American Drew	Central Park Lamps
American Impressions	Charles Sadek Imports
American Mirror	Charleston Forge
American Traditions	Classic Brass
Antigua, Inc.	Classic Leather
A.P.A.	Clayton Marcus
Ardley Hall Furniture	Clown Company
Art Concepts	C.M.S.
Arteriors	Cochrane Furniture
Artisian Art	Colonial Woodworks
Artistry	Comfortaire
Ashton Company	Cramco
Ashworth Art	Crawford
Aspen	Creative Expressions
Austin Sculpture	Crystal Clear
Baker Heritage	Decorating Delite
Barcalounger	Distinctive Design
Barclay Furniture	Eastern Accents
Bermex	Encore Creations
Bernards	Fifth Ave. Lighting
Brett Austin	Flexa Furniture
Broyhill	Floral Art
Bruards Furniture	Forturne Rattan

Franklin Reclining
Furniture Classics
Furniture Design
Furniture International
Furniture Traditions
Futuristic
Haeger
Hamilton Collections
Harper
Hickory Hill
Hickory Mark
Hickory Springs
Hooker Furniture
Hoyle
Hurtado
Imperial Rug
J. Royale
Jasper Cabinet
J.D.I.
Jenigere
Jennings
King Hickory
Kirby
Lane
Lea Furniture
Legend
Leisters Furniture
Lexington
Meadowcraft
Oak Hill Furniture
Oak Reflections
Oak-Wood
Ohio Table Pads
Omni Interiors

Ompei
Oriental Accents
Orleans Furniture
Outlook Furniture
Pacific Classic
Pacific Coast Lighting
Pacific Rim
Park Imports
Pennington Group
Peoplelounger
Phillips Collection
Progressive Furniture
Pulaski Furniture
Realistic Furniture
Relax-R Furniture
Ridgeway Clock
Ridgewood Furniture
River Forks
Riverside
Rossetto Furniture
Royal Designs
Rustic Designs
Sealy/Klaussner
Seascape Lamps
Serta
Shaw
Southern Living
Spring Air
Standard Furniture
Stanley Furniture
Steele Craft Lamps
Steele Creek
Stylecraft Furniture
T.L. Bayne

Thomasville	Waverly
Timeless Bedding	Wellington Hall
Universal Furniture	Wild Rose
Vaughan-Bassett	Windsor Art
Furniture	Woodlands Furniture
Vineyard	World Design
Virginia House	

Telephone/Internet orders accepted—payable by
    debit and Discover cards
Nationwide delivery
Size: 6,500 square feet
Payment policy: 50 percent down as deposit; check,
    cash, money order, or Discover; balance payable
    with any of above and MasterCard or Visa
Store manager: Tammy Davis

A main feature of this store is the focus on Klaussner's Dick Idol line: bedroom, living room, and dining
room suites in a rustic design in leather and fabric.
Though this is not one of the biggest Blowing Rock
stores (most of the Blowing Rock stores are concen-
trated in and around Hickory), you'll still be able to order
from the large number of manufacturers the company
carries and also reap the benefits of the volume sales
pricing. The manufacturers that Blowing Rock carries
tend to cater to modest-budget customers.

Carolina Furniture & Leather, Inc. (1st floor)
   (336) 454-1955
   (336) 454-8926
   Authorized dealer for, amongst others, Leather Mart,
      Martin Furniture, Homeland, Prima, Rivers Edge,
      Calia, and StrataLounger

Annual sales: March, September
Established: 1989
Size: 14,000 square feet
Number of sales staff: three (two with design educa-
    tion)
Telephone/Internet orders accepted
Nationwide delivery
Payment policy: Payment in full on in-stock items; 50
    percent down on custom orders, balance due be-
    fore shipping; cash, check, MasterCard, Visa, and
    Discover.
Store manager: Mike Smith

A wholesale and retail store that carries solid wood
bedrooms, dining rooms, and home office furnishings—
casual to formal. Also, as the name indicates, case
goods are not the only feature here—there are plenty of
options for leather and upholstery seating, too.

Decorator's Choice (1st floor)
    (336) 889-6115
    (336) 889-8656 (fax)
    E-mail: *decoratorschoice@atriumfurniture.com*
    Authorized dealer for Dinec, Trica, Vermont Preci-
        sion, Morlow, Morgan Stewart
    Annual sales: Dates are variable
    Established: 1990
    Size: 7,000 square feet
    Number of sales staff: two
    Telephone orders accepted
    Delivery through recommended carriers and in con-
        junction with other Atrium stores if possible

Payment policy: Visa, MasterCard, and personal
checks accepted; all orders must be paid in full
before shipping
Store manager: Sheila O'Reilly

With a wide selection of transitional and contemporary furniture, Decorator's Choice has a friendly staff
dedicated to helping you find the right furniture to suit
your personal look.

Fefco (4th floor)
(336) 882-0180
E-mail: *fefco@atriumfurniture.com*
Established: 1952, in Atrium since 1997
Size: 13,000 square feet
Number of sales staff: two
Telephone/Internet orders are accepted upon receipt
of deposit
Nationwide delivery with FEFCO-owned delivery
company; touchup man travels with furniture and
driver
Payment policy: One-third down as deposit, balance
due before delivery—which can be delayed for
up to one year if necessary; cash, checks, and all
major credit cards accepted
Store manager: Lina Hu

FEFCO—Far Eastern Furniture Company—manufactures all of its own furniture in China and features solid
kiln-dried hardwoods. Furniture is made from teak or
rosewood and is hand-rubbed with a Chinese lacquer
finish.

French Heritage Factory Store (1st floor)
(336) 884-0022
(336) 884-0020
www.frenchheritage.com
Authorized dealer for French Heritage
Annual sales: Same as Atrium calendar
Established: 1994 in Atrium; company since 1981
Number of sales staff: two
Nationwide delivery
Payment policy: Payment in full on floor samples, 50
    percent down on special orders; cash, check,
    Visa, and MasterCard accepted
Store manager: Lea Cooper

The designs of these reproductions of French antique furniture are carefully researched and painstakingly recreated to be an authentic "antiqued" product. Expect to find primarily floor samples, but special orders are available, too.

Kagan's (1st floor)
(336) 885-1333
Authorized dealer for Excelsior, Ello, Hooker, Rowe,
    Bassett, Broyhill, Ashley, American Drew, Carson's,
    Lazar, Legacy Leather, Johnston Casual,
    Millennium, and others
Established: 1988
Size: 18,000 square feet
Number of sales staff: four (one with formal design
    training)
Telephone/Internet orders accepted
Nationwide delivery

Payment policy: 50 percent down as deposit, balance
   due prior to shipping; cash and check accepted
Store manager: Mike Means

Contemporary and transitional manufacturers from
around the globe are the specialty of the house at
Kagan's 1st-floor store. Contemporary accessories and
sculptures accent the showroom floor and are also available to make your room complete.

Kagan's (3rd Floor)
   (336) 885-8300
   (336) 885-8307 (fax)
   E-mail: *kagans3atriumfurniture.com*
   Authorized dealer for Carlton Mclendon, Hooker,
      American Drew, Howard Miller, Bassett, Philip
      Reinisch
   Annual sales: January, May, July, and December
   Established: 1988, since the Atrium mall opened its
      doors
   Size: 3,645 square feet
   Number of sales staff: two (one with formal design
      training); eight in total in the Atrium
   Telephone orders are accepted
   Nationwide delivery
   Payment policy: 50 percent down as deposit, balance
      due before shipping
   Store manager: Leif Nordbladh

The three Kagan's galleries (total 18,000 square feet
and eight sales staff) have been in the Atrium Furniture
Mall since it opened its doors in 1988. This gallery specializes in traditional furniture and features dining room
and bedroom furnishings, curios, grandfather clocks,
and accent furniture.

Kagan's American Drew (2nd floor)
   (336) 885-8568
   (336) 885-8566 (fax)
   E-mail: *amdrew@atriumfurniture.com*
   www.kaganfurniture.com/americandrew
   www.kaganfurniture.com/canaldover
   Authorized dealer for American Drew and Canal
      Dover
   Annual sales: Variable from one year to the next
   Established: 1981
   Size: 1,150 square feet
   Number of sales staff: two (one with formal design
      education)
   Telephone/Internet sales are accepted
   National shipping available and work to coordinate
      with other Atrium stores if necessary and when
      possible
   Payment policy: 50 percent down as deposit, balance
      due upon arrival in warehouse.
   Store manager: Cecil Spencer

The concentration here is on showcasing the best and most popular selections of the American Drew and Canal Dover (made by the Amish) lines, which concentrate on traditional, Shaker, and country-style dining room and bedroom sets.

Kincaid Home Furnishings (2nd floor)
   (336) 883-1818
   (336) 883-1850 (fax)
   www.kincaidgalleries.com
   Authorized dealer for Kincaid, Laura Ashley Home,
      Serta, Artistica, Lloyd Flanders, California
      House, A.A. Lann, Barcalounger, Temple

Annual sales: September
Established: 1988
Size: 13,000 square feet
Number of sales staff: four (one with formal design
    education)
Telephone/Internet orders accepted as per individual
    manufacturer restrictions
Nationwide delivery
Payment policy: 50 percent down as deposit, balance
    due prior to shipping
Store manager: J.D. Winkler

Kincaid has been in the Atrium since the mall opened its doors and that is hardly the only feather in its cap: Kincaid is the largest solid wood manufacturer in the country and this store is the largest Kincaid dealer in North Carolina (and that's saying something). But there is also a lot more to this store than Kincaid case goods: There are also furnishings including Serta Bedding and Temple Upholstery.

Leather Land U.S.A. (4th floor)
    (336) 454-2215
    (336) 454-2811 (fax)
    E-mail: *leatherland@atriumfurniture.com*
    www.leatherland@atriumfurniture.com
    Authorized dealer for Elite, Legacy International,
        El-Ran, and Ashley
    Annual sales: May and November
    Store established: 1999
    Size: 6,500 square feet
    Number of sales staff: three (one with formal interior
        design education)

Telephone/Internet orders accepted
Nationwide delivery available and in conjunction
    with orders from other Atrium stores
Payment: 50 percent down as deposit, balance due
    before shipping; cash, check, Visa, MasterCard,
    and Discover accepted
Store manager: Nelson Bell

All of the furniture in Leather Land U.S.A. is upholstered in top-grain leather from some of the world's best
leather tanneries. Bench-made furniture is constructed
with a kiln-dried hardwood frame, eight-way hand-tied
springs, and comfortable durable cushions. The staff is
knowledgeable and can help you make heads or tails of
the different selections and quality levels.

Medallion Furniture (2nd floor)
    (336) 889-3432
    (336) 889-3433
    E-mail: *sales@contemporary-home.com*
    www.contemporary-home.com
    Authorized dealer for Nicoletti Leather, Far East Rat-
        tan, Grand Bay Upholstery, Jaymar Leather
    Annual sales: May, November
    Established: 1992
    Size: 7,200 square feet
    Number of sales staff: three (all with formal design
        education)
    Telephone/Internet sales accepted
    Nationwide delivery
    Payment policy: 50 percent down as deposit, balance
        due before shipping; Visa, MasterCard, American
        Express, Discover, and checks with proper ID
    Store manager: Jodi Glauber

Transitional to eclectic, contemporary to ultra-modern furnishings. If you have a taste for this style the highly trained sales staff (all have design education) can assist you in selecting the furniture that will work for your home.

Pennsylvania House (2nd floor)
(336) 886-5200
(336) 886-5204 (fax)
Authorized dealer for Pennsylvania House, Emerson, Wesley Alan, Mobel, Serta, and Cox
Annual sales: January and August
Established 1992
Size: 12,000 square feet
Number of staff: five (three with formal design education)
Telephone/Internet orders accepted
Nationwide delivery
Payment policy: 50 percent down as deposit, balance due before shipping; cash, check, Visa, MasterCard, and Discover accepted
Store manager: Carol Helms

The selection here includes American and traditional styles of bedroom, living room, and dining room furnishings in mahogany, oak, cherry, maple, and pine.

Also visit the Pennsylvania House Outlet on N. Main Street (see p. 188 for details).

➻Robert Bergelin Company (2nd floor)
(336) 889-2189
(336) 889-2190 (fax)
www.rbcfurn.com
Robert Bergelin furniture
Established: 1993

Size: 3,000 square feet
Number of sales staff: three
Telephone orders accepted
Nationwide shipping with in-home installation
Payment policy: 50 percent down as deposit, balance
    due before shipping
Store manager: Deb Keens

Truly artisanal in every regard, this case goods manufacturer is one of the "little guys" and everything is
factory-direct to you. Every order from Robert Bergelin is
handcrafted and designed especially for the customer
(from design preferences to the finish on the wood). It's
the sort of furniture that gets passed from one generation to the next. The tables are particularly beautiful, and
custom design requests of all kinds are accommodated.

Sina Oriental Rugs (3rd floor)
    (336) 885-7600
    (336) 885-2176 (fax)
    Specializing in handmade rugs, Oriental, and imported
    Annual sales: In conjunction with Atrium Mall sales
    In business since: 1982
    Size: 3,000 square feet
    Number of sales staff: two
    National shipping via U.P.S.
    Payment policy: Payment in full at time of purchase;
        cash, check, and credit cards accepted

This is the only rug gallery you'll find in the mall and
it's a good place to start—or finish—your grand shopping tour. The selection is substantial so be sure to take
advantage of the expert sales staff, who are available for
rug appraisals, too.

Wood-Armfield (see p. 101 for detailed listing)

> "Wear comfortable shoes, bring a pad and pen, a tape measure, a digital camera, your laptop computer. Bring floor plans, swatches, and paint chips. Bring photos of anything you already have that you're working around. Bring a suitcase on wheels if you have a lot of things to carry." —CHRISTINA RHEIN, VETERAN SALESWOMAN, BLACK'S FURNITURE

Special Nonfurniture Store Listings

⇥ **Abu Oriental Rugs**
  5626 Riverdale Drive (at stoplight on Business 85, next
    door to Furnitureland South, across the highway from
    Boyles)
  (336) 454-7771
  (336) 454-2329
  E-mail: *abuorientals@northstate.net*
  www.abuorientalrugs.com
  Hours: 9:00 AM–6:00 PM Monday–Saturday, Friday until
    8:30 PM; closed Sunday and major holidays
  Featuring rugs from India, Pakistan, Persia, Tibet, and
    China
  Annual sales: December
  Established: 1995
  Size: 7,000 square feet
  Number of sales staff: three
  Telephone orders accepted
  Nationwide delivery
  Payment policy: Payment in full at time of purchase;
    cash, check, American Express, Discover, Visa, and
    MasterCard

Abu's family has a long history in the rug business and
between the selection and the attentive and helpful sales staff

it is clear that to Abu, this isn't just a business but a matter of personal pride. It's not just about buying a "pretty rug" but about buying the right rug for your style and needs.

Alan Ferguson Associates
422 S. Main Street
(336) 889-3866
(336) 889-6271 (fax)
Hours: 9:00 AM–5:00 PM Monday–Friday, 10:00 AM–4:00
    PM Saturday; closed Sunday and major holidays
Authorized dealer for dozens of manufacturers including:
    Accessories International, Ambience, Dale Tiffany,
    Ello, Fabrica Rugs, Ferguson Copeland, Design Insti-
    tute of America, George Kovacs, Lorts, Maitland-
    Smith, Swaim, Mila International Glassware, Thayer
    Coggin, Theodore Alexander, and Van Teal

Alan Ferguson specializes in the unique. Expect to find one-of-a-kind pieces and the price tags to match (it's hard to place a price on a one-of-a-kind item, though because of the general competition, prices are still arguably lower than you would find at home). Selections include not just furnishings but also lighting, art, accessories, and drapery and upholstery fabrics.

Arts by Alexander
701 Greensboro Road
(336) 884-8062
(336) 884-8064 (fax)
Hours: 8:30 AM–5:00 PM Monday–Friday, 9:00 AM–
    1:00 PM Saturday, closed Sunday and major holidays
Authorized dealer for Bassett Mirror, Bradington Young,
    Cebu, Crawford, Braxton Culler, Oriental Accents,
    Oriental Lacquer, Thayer Coggin, Decorative Crafts,
    silver, and imports

Annual sales: Ongoing

Established: 1927 as Rhodes Press, since 1955 under current name and ownership

Size: 10,000 square feet in showroom space, 17,000 feet total

Number of sales staff: five employees

Telephone orders: Orders in writing are preferred

Store manager: Mary Fay Bodenheimer

A family owned business with a long history of unique furnishings and accessories. The emphasis is on accent and occasional pieces and custom picture framing.

➻ **Butler's Electric Supply, Inc.**

4380 Regency Drive, one mile south of I-40 off Highway 68

(336) 889-2344

(336) 889-2757

Hours: 7:30 AM–4:30 PM Monday–Friday, 8:30 AM–12:30 PM Saturday; closed Sunday and major holidays

Stocks 50 brands of lighting fixtures; represents and orders from over 100 brands; each manufacturer has on average a 2,000-item catalog, so that's over 200,000 lighting options to choose from

Annual sales: Continuously; there are always some close-outs on the floor

---

"Furniture is like a living thing—a color will vary on wood the way makeup would vary on a person." —CHARLIE GREENE, MANUFACTURER, CLASSIC GALLERY

Established: 1948, this location since 1991
Size: 10,000 square feet of showroom space, and grow-
ing; 18,000 square feet of stock
Number of sales staff: Variable, six to nine
Telephone orders accepted with deposit
Nationwide delivery
Payment: Deposit required, payable in cash, check, Visa,
MasterCard, or Discover
Store manager: Carlos Butler

By far the most comprehensive and cutting-edge lighting
selection I've ever encountered, Butler's has an extremely
knowledgeable and friendly staff on the ready to answer all of
your lighting questions. The concentration of stock is in high-
end products including one-of-a-kind antiques, crystal, and
European reproductions, and that's where you should expect
to save big over shopping in your area stores at home. Butler's
stays ahead of the trend curve by attending Market and stock-
ing the latest styles. Butler's—"if it lights up, we've got it"—
is also a full electric supply store and a family business.

✦ Gibson Interiors
1628 S. Main Street (first showroom to the left inside
Kagan's National Home Furnishings Building)
(800) 247-5460, (336) 883-4444, (336) 889-4939
(336) 883-0417
E-mail: *gibint@aol.com*
www.gibsoninteriors.com
Hours: 9:00 AM–6:00 PM Monday–Saturday, closed Sun-
day and major holidays
Annual sales: Regular markdowns throughout the year
Established: 1983
Size: 5,000 square feet
Number of sales staff: four

Telephone/Internet sales accepted
Payment policy: Payment upon purchase, cash, check,
  Visa, and MasterCard
Store Manager: Jim Gibson

Gibson Interiors is a worthwhile stop if only for the whimsy
of the furniture and accoutrements you'll find here. Originally
a lamp store, the stock of Gibson evolved naturally to emphasize the accessory, rather than the furniture, side of the market. Where else might you find a full-size Egyptian mummy
sarcophagus *cabinet*? Or perhaps it's the antique Chinese chess
set intricately carved from ivory that catches your eye. A little too much for your bungalow in Boca? The pink flamingo
neon lamp should be just the right accent to impress. The
stock is collected from furniture and accessory shows around
the country, antique shows along the East Coast, and international travels around the globe. The staff is knowledgeable
and genuinely friendly (no commissions are paid at Gibson so
even if you're the suspicious type, you can rest assured that
there's no hustling going on here) so whether you buy or not
you'll feel welcome.

Randall Tysinger Antiques

609 National Highway
Thomasville, North Carolina 27360
(336) 475-7174
(877) 524-0080
(336) 475-5604 (fax)
www.randalltysinger.com

Randall Tysinger, with stores in Thomasville, High Point,
and New York City, is one of the world's finest antique dealers, with one of the largest inventories in the business. The
Thomasville store is the flagship, and it is as amazing to visit

"If you're coming to buy end tables, measure the height of your sofa—you don't want tables that will be down at your ankles or up at your chin." —JANE EARNEST, MARKETING DIRECTOR, HICKORY FURNITURE MART

as any museum. Most people won't be able to afford anything at Randall Tysinger, but it's worth a stop in if you're anywhere nearby.

↠ **Replacements, Ltd.**
1089 Knox Road
Greensboro, NC 27420
(336) 697-3000
(800) REPLACE
E-mail: *inquire@replacements.com*
www.replacements.com

In Greensboro, just a short drive from High Point, is the greatest collection of china, silver, and crystal in the world. They carry more than 165,000 patterns, and if they don't have it or can't get it, it probably doesn't exist. The staff is tremendously helpful, knowledgeable, and friendly, and it's a fun place to visit whether you're replacing one missing piece of a pattern, buying all new merchandise, or just browsing.

Seagrove Pottery Center

Though not entirely convenient to High Point, if you're in the mood for a day trip and you need pottery you should consider an expedition to Seagrove. This is one of the nation's pottery capitals, and is well worth a visit. For more information and directions see *www.ncpotterycenter.com* or call (336) 873-8430.

Upton's Carpet & Rug Gallery
1111 S. Main Street
(800) 628-4621
(336) 886-4937
(336) 886-7837 (fax)
E-mail: *uptons@northstate.net*
www.uptonsrugs.com
Hours: 10:00 AM–5:00 PM Monday–Saturday; closed
   Sunday and major holidays
Authorized dealer for, amongst others, Karastan, Couris-
   tan, Fabrica, Glen Eden, Shaw, Bellridge Carpets,
   The Rug Market, Colonial Mills, Waverly carpets,
   and Oriental Weavers
National and international delivery
Payment policy: Payment in full upon purchase; cash,
   check, MasterCard, Visa, and Discover

Upton's is a comprehensive shopping destination for all of
your floor covering needs, whether it be rugs, wall-to-wall
carpeting, or hardwood or laminate flooring. Rugs range from
cotton throws to handmade silks. Covering floors for over 45
years, Upton's doesn't rest on its laurels and not only main-
tains an experienced sales staff but also offers customers the
opportunity to consult with a designer (a 25-year veteran) to
assist with all areas of design including coordinating the big
picture.

Zaki Oriental Rugs
600 S. Main Street
(336) 884-4407
(336) 884-5087 (fax)
E-mail: *Philip@zaki.com*
www.zaki.com
Hours: 9:00 AM–6:00 PM Monday–Saturday, closed Sunday and major holidays

Over 12,000 hand-knotted rugs from Pakistan, India,
   Iran, Turkey, Nepal, Egypt, and Afghanistan.
Annual sales: No sales, the lowest price is *always* marked
Established: 1977
Size: 100,000 square feet
Number of salespeople: five (two with formal interior
   design education)
Telephone/Internet orders accepted
Nationwide delivery
Payment policy: Payment in full upon purchase
Store manager: Jameel Khalifa

In addition to the extensive selection of hand-knotted rugs
from around the globe and the experienced sales staff, Zaki
also offers written appraisals, consultations for appraisal,
cleaning, repair and restoration, and even home trials. The
staff will also work with you to ensure compatibility with your
home and furniture purchases. Philip Thrift is a particularly
helpful salesperson.

Nearby Thomasville

Thomasville Furniture Factory Outlet
401 E. Main Street
Thomasville
(336) 476-2211
Hours: 9:00 AM–5:30 PM Monday–Friday, 9:00 AM–
   4:00 PM Saturday; closed Sunday and major holidays

The Thomasville name is perhaps one of the most recognized brands amongst furniture shoppers. Though Thomasville restricts retailers on discounting their furniture more than
a certain percentage, the outlets—which are selling market
samples and factory closeouts and are run by the company—
don't have the same restrictions. Here, as with all outlets, it's hit

or miss, no returns, and what you see is what you get—but when you do hit, you'll likely be saving big off the manufacturer's suggested retail price. In addition to Thomasville brand furniture you might also see pieces from Hickory Chair, Highland House, Pearson, and Hickory Business furniture—all part of the Thomasville furniture empire.

Thomasville makes excellent furniture—I have five pieces in my home—but I strongly disapprove of the way the company does business. They know they've got a good thing going, so they call the shots: Thomasville furniture is the least discounted furniture at the big High Point retailers because the company dictates prices and will pull its line from any store that doesn't toe the line. And the company has been very restrictive about telephone orders, another practice I find objectionable. Still, the values at the outlets cannot be denied.

NOTE: There are several Thomasville outlets (see below), and this is my least favorite. I found the space to be crowded and unpleasant to shop, the stock random, and the sales staff discourteous.

Also visit the Thomasville outlets in Greensboro (1410 Westover Terrace; (336) 273-2713; hours: 9:30 AM–6:00 PM Monday–Friday, 9:30 AM–5:00 PM Saturday; closed Sunday and major holidays) and Hudson (see Hickory Chapter listings on Route 321) for more Thomasville furniture savings.

ACCOMMODATIONS

Accommodations in High Point are for the most part strictly business: You'll find a preponderance of functional, basic hotels and motels that provide a place to sleep and a base from which to shop. There are three local hotels, however, that deserve special notice for providing above-and-beyond lodg-

ing experiences, and they are indicated by an ⊷. They are:
The J.H. Adams Inn, which is a beautiful, opulent historical
property; the Radisson, which is the most useful hotel in the
area; and the quirky, delightful Toad Alley Bed & Bagel, a historic home made over into a B & B by local designers.

NOTE: In addition to accommodations in High Point proper,
   you will find a wide variety of chain accommodations
   along the route from the Greensboro Airport to High
   Point. Although you'll have to drive a bit farther to get
   from these places to most of the major furniture stores,
   it's not a big deal if you're planning to spend all day
   shopping. And sometimes the High Point places book
   up, whereas there's almost always a room somewhere
   around Greensboro. Check in with the Greensboro
   Convention and Visitors Bureau for details on
   Greensboro-area lodging: (800) 344-2282
   (www.greensboronc.org).

Ashford Suites
3901 Sedgebrook Drive
High Point, NC 27265
(336) 812-8787
(336) 812-8788 (fax)
www.ashfordsuites.com
3 miles to airport, 7 miles to Downtown
80 Suites
Two-person Jacuzzi, fireplace, stereo, coffeemaker,
   microwave, stocked minibar, hairdryer, speakerphone,
   large work stations, indoor pool, outdoor patio, state-
   of-the-art exercise facility, evening reception, business
   centers, airport and surrounding area shuttle, deluxe
   continental breakfast, Alibi's Cafe & Club, 1,632-
   square-foot meeting room

Atrium Inn
425 S. Main Street
High Point, NC 27260
(336) 884-8838; (888) 928-7486
(336) 885-4925 (fax)
www.atrium-inn.com
16 miles to airport, located Downtown
36 rooms
32″ television with remote, cable, movie channels, direct-
dial phone, free local calls, alarm clock, iron and
board in room, coffeemaker, hairdryer, PC/modem
access, outdoor pool, laundry services, dry cleaning
services, newspaper, group discount offers, children
stay free, no pets, Atrium Inn located across the street
in the Atrium Furniture Mall (no relation)

Biltmore Suites
4400 Regency Drive
High Point, NC 27360
(336) 812-8188; (888) 412-8188
(336) 812-8185 (fax)
www.biltmoresuiteshotel.com
3 miles to airport, 7 miles to Downtown
62 Suites
Television with remote, cable, movie channels, pay-
per-view movies, direct-dial phone, free local calls,
speakerphones, alarm clock, iron and board in room,
coffeemaker, hairdryer, minifridge, PC/modem access,
minibars, wet bar, Jacuzzi (in 19 rooms), exercise
room, laundry services, dry cleaning services, complimentary newspaper, group discount offers, children
stay free, complimentary airport shuttle, no pets,
complimentary coffee, complimentary continental
breakfast, two complimentary evening cocktails,

Alibi's Restaurant (lunch/deli), lounge, room service, secretarial services, audio visual, podium, flip charts/boards, on-site catering, two business centers

Crestwood Suites
2860 N. Main Street
High Point, NC 27265
(336) 886-5665; (887) 398-3633
(336) 419-2045 (fax)
www.crestwoodsuites.com
16 miles to airport, 5 miles to Downtown
137 Suites
Nonsmoking and smoking rooms available, rooms have fully equipped kitchen with full-size refrigerator, coffeemaker, stove top, microwave, with on-site laundry, PC/modem access, direct-dial phone, free local calls, voice mail service, television with remote, cable, movie channels, alarm clock, ironing board available, safety deposit box, no pets

Days Inn & Suites
120 S.W. Cloverleaf Place
High Point, NC 27263
(336) 885-6000; (888) 329-7466
(336) 885-1155 (fax)
www.daysinn.com
22 miles to airport, 2 miles to Downtown
60 Rooms
Television with remote, satellite, direct-dial phone (free local calls), alarm clock, safe in room, PC/modem access, outdoor pool, group discount offers, children under 13 stay free, no pets, complimentary coffee, complimentary continental breakfast

High Point Inn
400 S. Main Street
High Point, NC 27260
(336) 882-4103
(336) 882-9903 (fax)
www.highpointinn.ws
16 miles to airport, located Downtown
43 Rooms
Television with remote, cable, movie channels, pay-per-
view movies, direct-dial phone (free local calls),
PC/modem access, laundry services, complimentary
newspaper, no pets, complimentary coffee, complimentary breakfast

Howard Johnson
2000 Brentwood Street
High Point, NC 27263
(336) 886-4141; (800) 446-4656
(336) 886-5579 (fax)
www.hojo.com
12 miles to airport, 1 mile to Downtown
104 Rooms
Television with remote, cable, movie channels, satellite,
VCR, direct-dial phone (client pays for local calls),
alarm clock, iron and board in room, coffeemaker,
hairdryer, minifridge, PC/modem access, heated outdoor pool, laundry services, dry cleaning services,
complimentary newspaper, safety deposit box, group
discount offers, children stay free, company airport
shuttle, no pets, complimentary coffee, Studio
Restaurant (American), room service, secretarial
services, audio/visual, podium, flip charts/boards,
on-site catering

-+- **J.H. Adams Inn**
1108 N. Main Street
High Point, NC 27262
(336) 882-3267; (888) 256-1289
(336) 882-1920 (fax)
www.jhadamsinn.com
16 miles to airport, located Downtown
30 Rooms
Television with remote, cable, movie channels, direct-dial
phone, free local calls, alarm clock, iron and board in
room, coffeemaker, hairdryer, minifridge in some
rooms, high speed PC/modem access, electronic wake-
up calls, no pets, nonsmoking facility, state-of-the-art
fitness studio, business center, lounge, dry cleaning,
complimentary newspaper, complimentary coffee, complimentary breakfast, evening reception, on-site catering, 500-square-foot meeting space, two meeting rooms

Without a doubt the finest hotel in the area, the J.H.
Adams Inn would be a noteworthy hotel almost anywhere in
the world. Built in 1918 and designed in the Italian Renaissance style as a private residence for John Hampton Adams,
the hotel has been completely renovated. Listed on the
National Register of Historic Places, it offers all the architectural grandeur of the original structure, plus all the modern
conveniences of a contemporary hotel. Convenient to local
businesses and furniture galleries.

-+- **Radisson Hotel**
135 S. Main Street
High Point, NC 27260
(336) 889-8888; (888) 333-3333
(336) 889-8870 (fax)
www.radisson.com/highpointnc

15 miles to airport, located Downtown
252 Rooms
Television with remote, cable, movie channels, pay-per-
    view movies, direct-dial phone, voice mail service,
    alarm clock, iron and board, coffeemaker, turn-down
    service, PC/modem access, radio, heated indoor pool,
    whirlpool, exercise facilities, dry cleaning services,
    complimentary newspaper, safety deposit box, group
    discount offers, children stay free, pets allowed ($50
    nonrefundable deposit), complimentary in-room cof-
    fee, Jack's Steakhouse (American Continental),
    lounge, room service, secretarial services, audio/visual,
    podium, flip charts/boards, on-site catering, pet
    friendly

The Radisson is the major hotel in Downtown High Point,
used by most of the key conventions and business gatherings.
The staff does a terrific job of accommodating a large number of guests, and rooms are spacious, comfortable, and quiet.
An ultra-reliable hotel in the ultra-reliable Radisson chain.

➤➤ Toad Alley Bed & Bagel

1001 Johnson Street
High Point, NC 27262
(336) 889-8349
(336) 886-6646 (fax)
www.toadalley.com
16 miles to airport, located Downtown
7 Rooms
TV, VCR, and cable, nine-foot ceilings, guest phone
    available, central air, smoke-free establishment, full
    Southern breakfast

The quirkiest and most intimate place to stay in the area,
Toad Alley Bed & Bagel is housed in a lovely 1924 Victorian

home in High Point's historic Johnson Street district. Renovated in 1987 by designers Alan Ferguson and John Paulen, the building features everything from a wraparound front porch with swing, to rocking chairs, to private sitting areas. Offers great comfort and easy access to everything.

Travel Inn Express
2429 W. Green Drive
High Point, NC 27260
(336) 883-6101
(336) 841-6698 (fax)
24 miles to airport, 2 miles to Downtown
60 Rooms
Television with remote, satellite, direct-dial phone (free local calls), alarm clock, safe in room, PC/modem access, outdoor pool, laundry services, dry cleaning services, complimentary newspaper, group discount offers, children stay free, no pets, complimentary coffee, complimentary continental breakfast

Travelodge
200 Ardale Drive
High Point, NC 27260
(336) 841-7717; (800) 578-7878
(336) 886-1284 (fax)
20 miles to airport, 2 miles to Downtown
83 Rooms
Television with remote, movie channels, satellite, direct-dial phone (free local calls), outdoor pool, no pets, complimentary coffee, complimentary breakfast

DINING

The overwhelming majority of restaurants in and around High Point are chains or otherwise generic. There are, however, a few standouts indicated by an ➝. Although the listings here are as comprehensive as possible and provided for your convenience, I strongly encourage you to seek out the few places that try hard to provide a little bit of local flavor: The best restaurant in town for fine dining is, without contest, J. Basul Noble's. It's the one place to go for "big city" food in High Point. At the same time, don't miss breakfast at Carter Brothers, lunch at the Dog House, or barbecue at Kepley's.

Key:
  $ Dirt cheap
  $$ Inexpensive to moderate
  $$$ Moderate
  $$$$ Expensive

Please also see the Barbecue Guide, p. 153, for an explanation of the whys and wherefores of North Carolina's great contribution to world cuisine.

American-Continental

➝ **Act 1**
130 E. Parris Avenue, (336) 869-5614
$$$
One of the better restaurants in town.

Alibi's (Biltmore Suites)
4400 Regency Drive, (336) 812-8188
$$$

➝ **Atrium Café**
430 S. Main Street, (336) 889-9934
$$
Not the greatest restaurant in High Point, but one of the
  most useful for a quick bite. Right in the Atrium Mall

and within footsteps of all the major Downtown attractions.

Austin's
2448 N. Main Street, (336) 869-1600
$$

⤛ **Jack's (Radisson)**
135 S. Main Street, (336) 889-8888
$$$
One of the more active and enjoyable bar scenes.

Mulligan's (Ashford Suites)
3901 Sedgebrook Road, (336) 812-8787
$$$

Studio (Howard Johnson)
200 Brentwood Street, (336) 886-4141
$$$

VinTerra Bistro & Gourmet Market
3805 Tinsley Drive, Suite 101, (336) 887-0094
$$

Asian

China Capital Restaurant
2900 N. Main St. (336) 882-8888
$$

Dragon City
274 Eastchester Dr. (336) 869-2966
$$

Dragon Wok
1589 Skeet Club Road, Suite 130, (336) 885-8885
$$

Fuji Japanese Steakhouse
133 E. Parris Avenue, (336) 869-9000
$$$

Golden China Restaurant
1677 Westchester Dr. #157, (336) 886-1388
$$

Ishikawa Japanese
2620 S. Main Street, (336) 885-4886
$$$

Kaya Japanese
3925 Sedgebrook Drive, (336) 841-0669
$$$

Rasa Grill
3793-145 Samet Drive, (336) 841-1154
$$

Thai Chiang Mai
2209 N. Main Street, (336) 869-0908
$$

Barbecue

NOTE: Please see the Barbecue Guide, p. 153, for much more information about area barbecue.

Barbecue Specialist
736 W. Fairfield Road, (336) 431-4969
$

⇥ **Carter Brothers**
2305 N. Main Street, (336) 869-9948
$

A great place for Southern breakfast, though the barbecue at Kepley's is better.

Country BBQ
411 W. Fairfield Road, (336) 431-8978
$

Henry James Bar-B-Que
621 Greensboro Road, 2217 S. Main Street
(336) 884-8038
$

↠ **Kepley's Barbeque**
1304 N. Main Street, (336) 884-1021
$
The best barbecue in the area, lovingly smoked over real wood coals.

Cafeterias

↠ **K. & W. Cafeteria**
1661 Westchester Drive, (336) 886-4442
$$
Part of the terrific K. & W. cafeteria chain, if you haven't been to one of these places you really should check it out. It's like stepping back in time to an era of good, wholesome, simple, and economical American food.

L. & R. Restaurant
808 W. Ward Street, (336) 884-1909
$$

Casual/Family

Alex's House
1223 N. Main Street, (336) 885-4161
$$

Big E's Diner
2225 S. Main Street, (336) 889-7445
$$

Cities' Grill
2440 N. Main Street, (336) 869-7956
$$

Cleary's
2140 N. Main Street #105, (336) 882-0600
$$

Dawn's Café
1000 Baker Road, (336) 434-7063
$$

⤞ **Dog House Restaurant**
662 N. Main Street, (336) 886-4953
$

A Downtown High Point institution, noted for its piled-
high frankfurters and fried bologna sandwiches. Also
just a lot of fun to visit.

K.C.'s Restaurant
2728 S. Main Street, (336) 883-4415
$$

Kim's Diner
1179 E. Lexington Avenue, (336) 882-2329
$$

Liberty Steakhouse & Brewery
914 Mall Loop Road, (336) 882-4677
$$$

Liz's Restaurant
2207 N. Centennial, (336) 889-0196
$$

Longhorn Steakhouse
1540 N. Main Street, (336) 883-7373
$$$

Main Street Grill
805 N. Main Street, (336) 887-2645
$$

Outback Steakhouse
260 E. Parris Avenue, (336) 885-6283
$$$

➤ **Panera Bread Bakery Café**
2400 Penny Road, (336) 812-4593
$
Good bread and light food items from this sourdough
bakery chain.

Peddler's Den
710 Ward Street, (336) 889-2606
$

Plaza Café
336 S. Main Street, (336) 886-5271
$$

Pomodoro
1345 N. Main Street, (336) 869-3514
$$

Rock-Ola Café
274 Eastchester Drive, (336) 887-8701
$$

Steak Street
3915 Sedgebrook Street, (336) 841-0222
$$$

Village Café
1141 E. Lexington Avenue, (336) 886-2233
$$

Coffee Shops

Debenn Expresso
709 W. Lexington Avenue, (336) 889-2107
$

Juice & Java
1231 Eastchester Drive, (336) 889-5952
$

Starbucks (Barnes & Noble)
906 Mall Loop Road, (336) 886-1331
$

See also Panera Bread, p. 145.

Deli

Best Bagels in Town
1116 Eastchester Drive, (336) 889-2700
$

Cajun Café and Blueberry Cool
921-2150 Eastchester Drive, (336) 886-6668
$

Capra's Deli
2640 Willard Dairy Road, (336) 454-5975
$

Cheesesteak Charly's
2900 N. Main Street, Suite 103, (336) 869-7784
$

Five Points Subs
1144 Five Points, (336) 886-4627
$

⊷ **Grateful Bread Baking Company**
1506 N. Main Street, (336) 884-4424
$
Good bread, and a good name.

Jersey Mike's Subs
2200 N. Main Street #103, (336) 885-3970
$

Mr. Gyro's
114 N. Elm Street, (336) 889-2489
$

Nick's Sub Shop
1102 W. Fairfield Road, (336) 861-5757
$

R. & R. Grill
2138 Surrett Drive, (336) 884-8212
$

Sub City Sandwich Shop
1014 S. Main Street, (336) 889-3359
$

Subway
1116 Eastchester Drive, 2501-D S. Main Street
(336) 869-7992
$

Family Dining

Big Ed's Chicken Pit
105 W. Peachtree Drive, (336) 869-7584
$$

Carolina's Diner
201 Eastchester Drive, (336) 869-0660
$$

Dinner Bell
2700 English Road, (336) 882-4568
$$

ᵗ˖ **Golden Corral**
1080 Mall Loop Road, (336) 884-1655
$$

Though the lunch and dinner buffets at the Golden Corral chain are mediocre, the restaurants put out a very good and reasonably priced weekend breakfast buffet. Great if you want to load up for the day and might be skipping lunch.

*"Utilize the people who are here to help you—sales staff, designers, mall information greeters. You're the reason they're here and they're expert at what they do." —*JANE EARNEST, MARKETING DIRECTOR, HICKORY FURNITURE MART

IHOP
110 E. Parris Avenue, (336) 869-3549
$$

➤ Rainbow Family Restaurant
1715 Westchester Drive, (336) 889-3133
$$
One of the most popular restaurants in the area, this is a good place to try some of the local Southern specialties. Nice corn bread.

➤ Rosa Mae's
106 N. Main Street, (336) 887-0556
$$
A downtown High Point institution; well worth a visit for honest cooking.

Sarah's Restaurant
800 W. Green Drive, (336) 887-7216
$$

Spiro's Family Restaurant
101 Coltrane Street, (336) 883-1390
$$

French

➤ J. Basul Noble's
101 S. Main Street, (336) 889-3354
$$$$
Called just Noble's by everyone, this is the premier fine-dining establishment in High Point and is widely regarded as one of the best restaurants in the region. The food is contemporary, with French, Italian, and New American accents, and the setting is spacious and elegant.

Italian/Pizza

Cici's Pizza
2705 N. Main Street #112, (336) 885-3333
$$

Elizabeth's Pizza
2505 Westchester Drive, (336) 889-4030
$$

George's Pizza
2505 N. Main Street #104, (336) 869-8645
$$

Gianno's Stone Oven Pizza
1124 Eastchester Drive, (336) 885-0762
$$

Pizza Hut
804 N. Main Street,
2749 S. Main Street, (336) 841-6114
$$

Pizza Inn
110 W. Fairfield Road, (336) 434-2138
$$

"When taking measurements on a piece of furniture remember that you not only have to get that table or sofa through your front door but you also have to maneuver it through your home— maybe around some corners or up a flight of stairs—and into the room you got it for." —RANDY GOOD, REGIONAL MANAGER, BOYLES FURNITURE

Pizza Vino
274 Eastchester Drive
2839 S. Main Street, (336) 885-5868
$$

Pizzeria Uno
3800 Sutton Way, (336) 884-4400
$$

Quizno's
3805 Tinsley Drive, (336) 885-4558
$$

Sir Pizza
1916 N. Main Street
2833 S. Main Street, (336) 841-6434
$$

Vino's Cafe
2850 S. Main Street, (336) 434-9682
$$

Latin/Mexican/Southwestern

Azteca Restaurant
712 S. Main Street, (336) 882-0066
$$

Cancun Mexican Restaurant
921 Eastchester Drive #1010, (336) 841-0983
$$

Chili's
920 Mall Loop Road, (336) 889-2505
$$

El Ranchito
2300 N. Main Street, (336) 869-3001
$$

La Hacienda
2826-A S. Main Street
1116 Eastchester Drive, (336) 841-6384
$$

Mi Pueblo
111 Northpoint Avenue, (336) 887-5518
$

Taqueria Las Cazuelas
1700 English Road, (336) 884-8428
$

Seafood

Libby Hill Seafood
2004 N. Main Street, (336) 882-4191
$$

P. & P. Seafood
1916 E. Green Drive, (336) 887-3172
$$

Sanibel's Seafood
2929 N. Main Street, (336) 841-6002
$$

Skipper's Seafood
2409 S. Main Street, (336) 885-8678
$$

BARBECUE GUIDE

Barbecue is the great indigenous cuisine of North Carolina, and it pays to learn a little bit about it before you set foot in the state. So, for those of you who aren't familiar with the ins-and-outs of North Carolina's unique barbecue tradition and culture (and make no mistake, it is a culture), here's a very brief (and, as a result, not fully nuanced) overview.

North Carolina is probably the most fanatical of all the states when it comes to barbecue. It's hard to imagine how seriously they take it, unless you go down and experience the passion.

The first thing to remember is that in North Carolina the word "barbecue" is a noun. It refers to a specific product, namely pork smoked over hardwood (usually hickory or oak) coals. In the modern era, gas-fired and electric cookers are used as well, but of course the purists reject them. You would not ever refer to the backyard grill as "a barbecue" the way it's done in most of America. People in North Carolina would think you're feeble-minded or don't speak very good English: Chicken thrown on your grill is not "barbecued chicken" in North Carolina. That's grilled chicken. Barbecue, as every self-respecting Southerner knows, is a noun.

Thing number two: North Carolina is split into Eastern North Carolina and Western North Carolina styles of barbecue (ENC and WNC is how the barbecue experts write it), and this is where it gets a bit confusing. Both styles are made from pork. But WNC style is pork shoulder only, whereas ENC style is the whole hog. Both are usually chopped, though you can get WNC style sliced as well. You won't typically see ENC style sliced, because it's the whole hog and the whole point is to chop it and mix the different types of meat together for the best result.

There is also a difference in the sauce, always applied after cooking (North Carolina barbecue is a dry style, meaning no sauce is applied during the smoking process, as opposed to the wet style you'll see at some rib places in Memphis). In WNC barbecue, you have a sauce with a bit of tomato in it. In ENC style, the sauce has no tomato. It's just vinegar and pepper, pretty much. There are some other differences as well, and they extend to the other things served with the barbecue, such as the coleslaw. WNC coleslaw is reddish, because it has some tomato in it, too. ENC slaw is white, like the normal coleslaw you see everywhere else in America.

Thing number three is that, while the East in ENC is East, the West in WNC actually refers to the Central part of the state, right around where High Point is. So when you say WNC you're not really talking about the Western part of the state, like over where Hickory is. In fact, there's not much serious North Carolina barbecue out in the true Western part of the state. That far West, the barbecue starts to show Tennessee influences and is a whole different ballgame. What a mess.

Thing number four is that you've got to understand a few unique local terms.

For example, there's "tea." This is the official beverage accompaniment to North Carolina barbecue and if you're not used to Southern-style tea it can be a bit of a shock. It's so sweet, you can't believe the liquid can support that much sugar dissolved into it. Of course you never say "iced tea." You just say "tea." That means you want iced tea with about one pound of sugar per cup of tea. If you want unsweetened iced tea, you can get it, but it's borderline rude to ask for it. In the event you do, however, be advised the word "unsweetened" is not part of the local English. The word in North Carolina is the delightfully elegant and almost Shakespearean "unsweet."

Then there's the sandwich versus the "plate" versus the "tray." You can get your barbecue on a bun sandwich, like a Sloppy Joe except with barbecue on it, in which case the bun contains chopped barbecue plus coleslaw right on the sandwich. You can get a tray, which is a rectangular cardboard tray with half barbecue and half coleslaw. Or you can get a plate, which is a three-sectioned cardboard plate with barbecue, coleslaw, and fries. Yes, the plate is bigger than the tray. Go figure. With both the plate and the tray you get a choice of rolls or hush puppies on the side. Get the hush puppies—little fried bits of cornmeal—for they are one of the world's great foods.

Where to Eat Barbecue Near High Point

If barbecue is your mission, you're pretty lucky to find yourself in High Point. Not only is there a world-class barbecue joint right in town (Kepley's), and not only is one of the most famous of all barbecue places right in nearby Greensboro (Stamey's), but also you're within a very short drive (about 20 minutes) of what many consider to be the center of the barbecue universe: Lexington, North Carolina. The town of Lexington is teeming every day of the year (except Sundays when many of the places are closed) with barbecue aficionados making pilgrimages to taste the work of the masters. Indeed, the WNC barbecue style is often just called

"If something arrives in your home and there's a little nick or scratch, give the company a chance to make it better. They'll send someone to fix it, someone who does this for a living and is a real pro. Having a touchup doesn't make your dining table or breakfront damaged goods. And I'll let you in on a little secret—even something that arrives in your home in "perfect" condition was almost certainly touched up in the factory before it shipped to you, but can you find it? No, you can't, and you shouldn't be able to recognize the spot after your in-home touchup either."
—DENIS RAINEY, RAINEY & ASSOCIATES, INC.

"Lexington style." Here are a few key barbecue addresses in Lexington. Each of these places is excellent, and choosing among them is mostly a matter of taste, plus the luck of the draw (barbecue is an artisanal product that varies greatly from day to day). Were it necessary to rank them, however, this would be one arguable hierarchy:

1. Cook's Barbecue
Valiant Drive, (704) 798-1928
Call for directions, because it's tough to find.

2. Lexington Barbecue #1
10 Highway 29-70S, (910) 249-9814

3. The Barbecue Center
900 N. Main Street, (704) 246-4633

4. Jimmy's Barbecue
1703 Cotton Grove Road, (704) 352-2311

5. Smokey Joe's Barbecue
1101 S. Main Street, (910) 249-0315

To get to Lexington from High Point, just take U.S. 311 South out of High Point and connect up with I-85 South. It will take you right in.

In Greensboro

Stamey's Old-Fashioned Barbecue
2206 High Point Road, Greensboro, NC
(910) 299-9888

In High Point

Kepley's Barbeque
1304 N. Main Street, (336) 884-1021

If you want to learn a lot more about barbecue, pick up the great little book, *North Carolina Barbecue: Flavored by Time*, by Bob Garner. It contains a guide to every top barbecue restaurant in the state, plus a lot more information that can be given here about the different styles, including ENC, WNC, pig pickin's, and more.

ATTRACTIONS

Although High Point is not a major tourism area—except insofar as furniture shopping is concerned—there are a number of enjoyable local attractions and activities from which to choose, especially if you're there for an extended trip. The furniture-related attractions are particularly relevant to those wishing to have the complete furniture shopping experience.

Angela Peterson Doll & Miniature Museum
101 W. Green Drive, (336) 885-DOLL (3655)
Monday–Saturday 10:00 AM–4:30 PM, Sunday 1:00 PM–
4:30 PM. Closed Monday November–March

Over 2,000 dolls, miniatures, and dollhouses. Special exhibit of over 130 Shirley Temple dolls and other rotating doll and miniature exhibits. Group guides available with reservation. One of the largest doll museums. Located next to the Furniture Discovery Center.

⤙ Bernice Bienenstock Furniture Library
1009 N. Main Street. (336) 883-4011
Monday–Friday 9:00 AM–12:00 PM and 1:00 PM–5:00 PM.

The Bienenstock Library has far and away the world's largest collection of books on the history of furniture. Tours available by appointment. Free admission.

➤➤ Furniture Discovery Center
101 W. Green Drive, (336) 887-3876
Monday–Friday 10:00 AM–5:00 PM, Saturday 9:00 AM–5:00 PM, and Sunday 1:00 PM–5:00 PM. Closed Monday November–March

This is a very worthwhile stop if you want to gain a deeper understanding of furniture. The museum is painstakingly organized and crammed full of information. Exhibits simulate a furniture factory and show various elements of the manufacturing process. There are several special exhibits and the museum is designed for hands-on appeal to all ages. Group guides available by reservation. Great gift/book shop. Located adjacent to Angela Peterson Doll and Miniature Museum.

High Point Museum & Historical Park
1859 E. Lexington Avenue, (336) 885-1859
Tuesday–Sunday, 10:00 AM–4:30 PM

A nice set of exhibits, including tours (by costumed guides) of the 1754 Hoggatt and 1786 Haley Houses. The museum focuses on the history of High Point with an emphasis on the

A display at the Furniture Discovery Center in High Point.

"Home Furnishings Capital of the World" theme. In addition to furniture, there are exhibits on textiles and transportation.

John Coltrane Commemorative Marker

This commemorative marker on the corner of Centennial Street and Commerce Avenue in High Point is located near the boyhood home of legendary jazz saxophonist John Coltrane (1926–1967). He grew up on Underhill Street and graduated at age 16 from William Penn High School.

McCulloch Gold Mill

6328 Kivett Loop, Jamestown, NC 27282
(336) 887-2206; (336) 887-3936 (fax)
E-mail: *info@mccullochfoundation.org*

You can pan for gold, and also take in various Earth sciences and North Carolina history exhibits. Off Interstate Business 85, south of Greensboro, in Jamestown.

Mendenhall Plantation

603 W. Main Street, (336) 454-3819
Tuesday–Friday 11:00 AM–2:00 PM, Saturday 1:00 PM–
    4:00 PM, Sunday 2:00 PM–4:00 PM. Other times by
    reservation.

This 19th-century Quaker plantation supported the abolitionist movement in the Civil War, and you can see a false-bottom wagon (one of only two remaining) that was used to transport slaves to freedom. Listed in the National Historic Register.

Millis Regional Health Education Center

601 N. Elm, (336) 888-6713
www.highpointregional.com

A fun interactive health education exhibit appealing to kids. You can measure your height against a full-size Michael Jordan, and more.

Museum of Old Domestic Life
555 E. Springfield Road, (336) 882-3054
This is a Quaker museum located in the 1858 Springfield Meeting House, displaying artifacts from colonial Quaker homesteads. Tours by appointment.

➤➤ North Carolina Shakespeare Festival
1014 Mill Street, (336) 841-2273
www.ncshakes.org

Shakespeare and other performances from August through October. There's also a special performance of Dickens' *A Christmas Carol* every December. Performances at the High Point Theater.

➤➤ North Carolina Zoological Park
4401 Zoo Parkway, Asheboro, NC 27203
Information: (336) 879-7000
www.nczoo.org

Located in Asheboro, the North Carolina Zoological Park is the world's largest natural habitat zoo. Among many other things, it features an African region with eight outdoor exhibits and more than 200 animals; the R.J. Reynolds Aviary with free-flying birds; and the wonderful warthog exhibit.

➤➤ Piedmont Environmental Center
1220 Penny Road, (336) 883-8531
Center: Monday–Saturday, 9:00 AM–5:00 PM, Sunday 1:00 PM–5:00 PM. Trails: Sunrise to sunset seven days a week
www.highpointnc.com/pec

Here you'll find 375 acres of hiking trails around the picturesque High Point City Lake, plus a nature preserve, gift shop,
and small animal and map exhibits. This is also where you gain
access to the six-mile Greenway Trail. Free admission.

Theatre Art Galleries
220 E. Commerce Ave. (in the High Point Theater
    building), (336) 887-2137
Monday–Friday 12:00 PM–5:00 PM, weekends by reser-
    vation; closed part of April and October

Rotating art exhibits in three galleries.

-*- World's Largest Chest of Drawers
508 N. Hamilton Street
(336) 883-2016

The name says it all. This building is actually shaped like a
chest of drawers, and it would be a crying shame to leave High
Point without taking a family photo in front of this behemoth.
It was built in 1926 to emphasize the "Home Furnishings
Capital of the World" theme that is so prevalent in High
Point. It was improved and restored as a four-story 18th-
century chest of drawers and is now the home to the High
Point Jaycees.

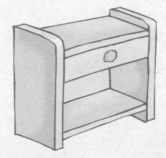

3

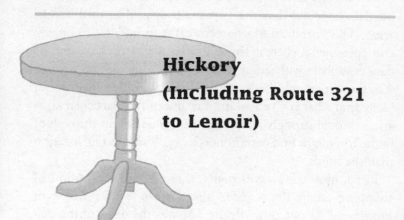

Hickory
(Including Route 321
to Lenoir)

The two primary shopping options in Hickory are the Hickory Furniture Mart and the Catawba Furniture Mall. Each of the two has a distinct personality: The Furniture Mart reminds me of one of those giant Galleria malls that were popping up all around the country in the 1980s. The Catawba Mall is more akin to your local mall; it has been around for decades and keeps up with the times by regular spruce-ups and improvements.

The primary difference between your malls at home and these two malls is that, here, the malls are 100 percent dedicated to furnishings and related items. Each is worthy of a visit. With so much furniture to choose from, there are of course overlaps in manufacturers (that is to be expected even from one store to the next regardless of where you shop), but I have found that the two malls specialize in different areas: The Furniture Mart stores cater to middle- to upper-end customers, whereas the Catawba mall stores accommodate customers with lower budgets and, although they range into the upper end, that's not the focus. In either mall, you'll likely find what you're looking for, but in this particular situation I would strongly encourage you to do a walk-through of both. You might find certain needs better met in one location than the other.

In addition to the two malls, there is also the option of shopping along Route 321, also known as "22 Miles of Furniture." At one time, Route 321 was the heart of the discount furniture shopping market. All of the Hickory furniture stores worth their salt were situated along this road; it was *the* place to come for furniture bargains. With the advent of the Hickory Furniture Mart and the Catawba Furniture Mall, the business gradually shifted from shopping the individual stores along Route 321 to the convenience and ease of the mall environment. Now, most shoppers to Hickory never bother to strike out beyond the two furniture malls—and as time goes on there's less and less reason to do so. Unless you're looking to shop some of the outlets that aren't in the Mart (of which there are a few on and nearby 321), or you're looking for a lower price point (there's a lot of good but inexpensive furniture along 321), your time is better spent at the malls.

If you're coming to Hickory to shop for furniture, you've most likely chosen it for the convenience of the mall experience. Otherwise, you'd probably have gone to High Point. Therefore, shopping the stores on 321 essentially offers the worst of the two towns: No mall convenience (because you have to drive from store to store), smaller selection (because for the most part the stores on 321 are not nearly as large as the stores in High Point), and too many disreputable stores selling junk. This does not mean you can't get great furniture bargains along Route 321, or that every store is here today and gone tomorrow. Bonita Furniture Galleries has been around for years and has many satisfied customers. Furthermore, the stores along Route 321 have open distribution from manufacturers—any store can carry any manufacturer so long as the store meets the manufacturer's approval—unlike those in the malls where the stores are often competing for manufacturer lines.

The majority of this chapter focuses on the Hickory Furniture Mart and the Catawba Furniture Mall; however, also included is a section on Route 321 and the bargains to be found there. In addition, the chapter includes key information about lodging, dining, and attractions in and near Hickory.

NOTE: If you do decide to shop along Route 321, be sure that the stores you buy from are reputable and legitimate. It is critical that before you plunk *any* money down, you check in with the Better Business Bureau and the Chamber of Commerce for a thumbs-up. This is also good advice regardless of where you decide to shop, for furniture or anything else, anywhere.

HICKORY FURNITURE MART

2220 Highway 70 S.E.
(828) 322-3510
(800) 462-MART
www.hickoryfurnituremart.com
Hours: 9:00 AM–6:00 PM Monday–Saturday; closed Sunday, January 1, July 4, Thanksgiving, December 24 & 25
Established: 1985
Size: 20 acres of furniture shopping—over one million square feet

Number of stores: 40

Shipping: Unless otherwise specified, all purchases in the
Mart can be shipped through the Mart Shipping Association: (800) 874-6486; (828) 431-4766; (828) 431-
4765 (fax); orders from multiple stores can be
consolidated and shipped at the combined freight
weight charge

One thousand manufacturers are represented throughout the
40 stores and 100 galleries in the Furniture Mart. The main
entrance is the South entrance where there is an information
desk with Mart directories and a greeter who will gladly
answer all of your questions. The West entrance has a visitor
center and all of the same resources that the South entrance
offers (plus brochures on regional attractions).

You can rest easy when you shop the Mart because the Mart
itself is a member of the Better Business Bureau and the
Chamber of Commerce, and a great majority of the stores are,
too. Not only does the Mart have a longstanding reputation
but so do most of the stores in the Mart, and everyone
involved in your experience will work to make sure you have
a positive experience from beginning (when you enter the
Mart and each of the stores) to end (when the furniture arrives
in your home).

Some of the conveniences of shopping at the Hickory
Furniture Mart include the Hickory Coffee Company on
Level 1, at which I became a regular during my long tenure
in Hickory and which, I am certain, saved my life with regular infusions while I was there. It offers the best (and one of
the only serious) cups of coffee in town. For those who are less
impressed by and addicted to coffee, the friendly folks at the
coffee joint also sell baked goods, cold drinks, and other
treats. For lunch, aside from the selection at the Coffee
Company, Jessica's Veranda, located on Level 2, offers sand-
wiches and other lunch fare. The Mart is handicapped-

accessible and wheelchairs are available for customers who need them. A shuttle service is also available from any Mart entrance to your car via the "Mart Cart." And perhaps my favorite of all: Pagers are available on loan for families (or anyone else) wanting to split up but stay in touch. Let me clue you in on a little secret: Many husbands, after reaching their shopping limits, make a beeline for Applebees (across the Mart parking lot) and camp out in front of the big-screen TVs at the bar until wives page them at times of critical decision-making.

NOTE: Each store has its own payment schedule but, if not specified, it is safe to assume that the store requires one-third to one-half of the purchase total down as a deposit and the balance due *before* shipping.

Mart Shipping Association

(800) 874-6486
(828) 431-4766

The pressing questions of how to ship your furniture after purchases have been made and if (and how) you can consolidate purchases from different stores within the Mart are legitimate concerns to consider before you begin to buy. For those of us accustomed to paying big bucks to ship a single piece of furniture a couple of miles, it will come as a great relief (and surprise) to find that not only has the Mart Shipping Association taken all of the guesswork and worry out of an often confusing proposition—getting your furniture from here to there—it also contracts with reliable shippers who are reasonably (and competitively) priced. All freight costs are based upon a permutation of weight and distance. The more you ship, the less per pound you pay. All of the stores in the Mart, with the exception of Boyles, ship through the Mart

> *"When buying counter and bar stools, you'll want seating that is 6–8 inches lower than your counter height, measured from the floor up to the bottom of your counter."* —STEFANI BEANE, STORE MANAGER, LIFESTYLES FURNITURE

Shipping Association. When you check in at one of the visitor desks in the Mart, paperwork, including an information sheet and shipping form, are available. There is also a Mart Shipping Association office located on Level 4 by the South entrance. Feel free to stop in there with questions (the split shipping forms have to be dropped off to the office *before* you leave the Mart) or give them a call.

Designing Women, Inc. (Level 3)
(828) 328-5200
(828) 328-5560

Sally Bently is the owner and one of the designers at Designing Women, located right in the Hickory Furniture Mart for your convenience. Sally or one of her team can work with you for a few hours or a few days to help you take the guesswork out of furnishing your home during whatever amount of time you have to spend in Hickory. It's best to make an appointment in advance if you know you want the help of a designer or even if you just want to have the practiced eye and years of experience of a professional to show you the ropes. The designers at Designing Women will take the edge off and turn your shopping experience into an entertaining adventure (if you don't laugh until you cry while working with Sally; well, I most certainly did). It's a reasonably priced $50 per hour with a three-hour minimum or $350 for an entire long day. I had the opportunity to meet a few of Sally's clients and one couple (which had engaged Sally for the previous two days to help furnish a vacation home in Florida) went so far as to say that she "thanked God at night for finding Sally" and for the help that Sally had provided during their shopping excursion in Hickory. If that's not high praise, I don't know what is.

Amish Oak & Cherry
(828) 261-4776
(828) 261-4779
www.amishoakandcherry.com
Authorized dealer for, amongst others, Oakwood Interiors and Brentwood
Annual sales: January, February, May, June, July, August, November
Established: 1998
Size: 5,000 square feet
Number of sales staff: two
Telephone/Internet orders accepted
National delivery
Payment policy: 25 percent down as deposit, balance due before shipping; cash, checks, MasterCard, and Visa accepted
Store manager: Misty Bumgarner

Just like the name says, the furniture here is Amish and it's all handcrafted from solid oak and cherry. Eight oak and four cherry finishes are available to personalize your selection. An extensive finish (15 steps they say) is part of the construction on every piece which promises to be resistant to scratches, spills, and stains.

Basset Furniture Direct (Level 2)
(828) 267-0670
(828) 267-0843 (fax)
Authorized dealer for Bassett furniture

Annual sales: February, November
Established: 1999 retail store in the Mart, company established in 1902
Size: 14,000 square feet
Number of sales staff: six (two with formal design education)
Telephone/Internet sales are accepted
Payment policy: 25 percent down as deposit, balance due upon receipt of goods in warehouse; cash, check, American Express, Discover, MasterCard, and Visa accepted; financing is available with the "Bassett card"
Store manager: Kathy Willson

If you know you want Bassett furniture this is where you'll want to start. The store showcases the world's largest selection of Bassett's most popular styles, all of which can be special ordered from the factory. Because of Bassett's relationship with the factory, custom upholstered orders from this store can be processed in 30 days from order (unlike the 8–12 weeks to delivery from other stores). And you'll also find all of the full-service trappings here—from special orders to help with interior design—as you would at the other large stores.

Boyles Galleries (Level 4)
(828) 326-1748
(828) 326-1799 (fax)
store5@boyles.com
Authorized dealer for 27 manufacturers including Henkel Harris, Hickory Chair, Hickory White, Cox, Bradington Young, Kindel
Annual sales: February
Established: 1985; this is the oldest store in the Furniture Mart; Boyles opened its first store in 1949 and has subsequently opened 11 others in North Carolina
Size: 25,000 square feet

Number of sales staff: 16 (2 with formal design education)

Telephone orders are accepted as per individual manufacturer restrictions

National delivery by Classic Moving and Storage, exclusively available to Boyles customers

Payment policy: One-third down as deposit by check, MasterCard, or Visa; balance due in certified funds upon delivery

Store manager: Jerre Rhoney

You won't see many more tastefully designed showrooms than those at Boyles. Each of the four Boyles stores in the Mart features medium- to high-end manufacturer's lines arranged attractively in mixed showrooms simulating an "in home" feel, as well as galleries dedicated to showcasing individual manufacturers. You'll find it all here—dining rooms to dens, cottage to formal furnishings—and you can complete each look with accessories, too. Each Boyles store features and showcases different manufacturers so it's good to visit all four and see which manufacturers best cater to your needs and taste. And it all arrives to your home under the professional watch and care of Classic Moving & Storage, exclusive to Boyles and specializing in white-glove service (literally). Custom orders available.

➤ **Boyles Showcase** (Levels 2 & 3)
(828) 326-1735
(828) 326-1758 (fax)
www.boyles.com
store10@boyles.com
Authorized dealer for 44 manufacturers including Henredon, Bernhardt, Hooker, Century, Hancock & Moore, Sherrill, Stanley, Ralph Lauren, Harden, Marge Carson, Kingsdown, and Nichols & Stone

Annual sales: February, July
Established: 1987
Size: 54,000 square feet
Number of sales staff: 22 (two with formal design education)
Telephone orders accepted as per individual manufacturer restrictions
National delivery with Classic Moving and Storage
Payment policy: One-third down as deposit by check, MasterCard, or Visa; balance due in certified funds upon delivery
Store manager: Randy Good

See Boyles Galleries, page 170, for details.

Broyhill Showcase Gallery (Level 4)
(828) 324-9467
(828) 324-4219
Authorized dealer for Broyhill, Serta
Annual sales: February, July, and after Market sales in May, November
Established: 1989
Size: 10,000 square feet
Number of sales staff: three
Telephone orders accepted
Payment policy: Cash, check, MasterCard, and Visa accepted

Envision what you want your living room to look like, and voilá! At this Broyhill showcase there are galleries full of livable and comfortable rooms set up as if they were in a home— giving you a realistic idea of how the furnishings will look in *your* home. It's a comfortable and friendly atmosphere, and the salespeople are very experienced and happy to help. Don't be afraid to ask all of your questions. Custom orders available.

Century Fabric Outlet (In Mart complex, a separate
   building, behind Holiday Inn Express)
(828) 324-5199
Hours: 9:00 AM–6:00 PM Monday–Saturday; closed Sun-
   day and major holidays
Authorized dealer for Century and Councill fabrics
Established: 2000
Size: 5,000 square feet
Number of sales staff: three

This store is the *only* authorized Century and Councill fabric outlet. You can buy a piece or the entire roll. Selections
include fabric, leather, hides, and frames.

Century Factory Outlet by Hollin Gate (Level 4)
(828) 324-2442
Authorized outlet for Century, Councill, Hickory Chair
Annual sales: February, July
Established: 1985, first Hollin Gate store in 1974
Size: 22,000 square feet
Number of sales staff: three
Telephone orders accepted but products are being sold
   off the floor "as is" so telephone purchases are sight-
   unseen
Payment policy: Payment in full upon purchase of goods;
   cash, check, and bank card accepted

If you're interested in Century and Councill brands, this
store is a real find. It's the only store authorized to sell the
closeouts.

➤➤ **Comfort Zone by Hickory Park** (Level 3)
(828) 326-9224
(828) 323-1997 (fax)
Authorized dealer for Lane, Berkline, Barcalounger,
   Keller, Woodard, and Lloyd Flanders

Annual sales: February
Established: 1994
Size: 13,000 square feet
Number of sales staff: three
National delivery
Payment policy: One-third down as deposit payable by
    cash, check, MasterCard, and Visa; balance due by
    check or certified funds
Store manager: Douglas Shannon

If it's motion furniture you want, the Comfort Zone is certainly a good place to start your search. You'll see the top brands, whether you're looking for recliners, incliners, reclining sofas, or reclining sectionals. The adjoining "Seasons" Outdoor Gallery features a wide selection of outdoor furniture including rattan and wicker.

Councill Factory Outlet by Hollin Gate (Level 4)
(828) 324-2442

See Century listing, p. 173, for details

DonLamor, Inc.
(828) 324-1776
(828) 324-1676 (fax)
donlamor@twave.net
www.donlamor.com
Authorized dealer for Vanguard, Leathercraft, Lee Industries, Swaim Classics, Lorts, French Heritage
Annual sales: February, May, August, November
Established: 1987
Size: 16,000 square feet
Number of sales staff: six (two with formal design education)

Telephone/Internet orders accepted as per individual
manufacturer restrictions

National delivery

Payment policy: 50 percent down as deposit, balance due
upon delivery (if delivered by a commercial carrier
that specializes in fine furniture, final payment must
be made prior to delivery); cash, check, Visa, and
MasterCard are accepted

Store manager: Steve McNeely

The fourth tenant in the mall, DonLamor has staying power and it isn't difficult to see why. The selection of furnishings is unique: You'll find smaller niche manufacturers with products you won't see everywhere else. This gives the store (and your home) a unique and individual feel. The sales staff is there to help you find the right look for your home, whether that means matching sets (or suites) or mixing and matching (which is encouraged).

"Before you make the trip to North Carolina, do some shopping around. Call a few stores and make some price comparisons to determine if the trip is going to be worthwhile for you. But be sure you're comparing apples to apples. When comparing prices, look to see that you've got the same manufacturer, the same item, and the same fabric or finish—otherwise you're just comparing two similar items that look the same, one of which may be of substantially lesser quality, and that of course will affect the price. If Ford had a model that looked like a Rolls-Royce, would it be the same quality car or would it just look similar?"
—STEVE NOBLE, GENERAL MANAGER AND VETERAN SALESMAN, HOME FOCUS FURNITURE

Drexel Heritage Factory Outlet (Level 1)
(828) 324-2200
(828) 323-8445 (fax)
Authorized dealer for Drexel Heritage, Maitland-Smith, and La Barge
Annual sales: January, February, May, November
Established: 1994
Size: 20,000 square feet
Number of sales staff: three (one with formal design education)
Telephone orders are accepted
Payment policy: Payment in full upon purchase; cash, check, American Express, Visa, and MasterCard are accepted
Store manager: Trish Triggs

A factory outlet in the true sense of the word, the Drexel Heritage outlet has a continuously evolving stock of showroom samples, discontinued items, and slightly imperfect furniture. If this is your kind of furniture—and these are certainly considered excellent brands—this is the place in the mall to start because if you see something you like here, you won't find it elsewhere for a better price. No custom orders available.

Ferguson-Copeland/Theodore Alexander/Hickory White Factory Outlet (Level 4)
(828) 327-3766

See listing under Hickory White Factory Outlet, page 180, for details.

➳ **Flexsteel Gallery by Hickory Park** (Level 2)
(828) 322-4440
(828) 326-9678 (fax)

Authorized dealer for Flexsteel, Master Design, Artistica,
and Regency House
Annual sales: February, May, November
Established: 2001
Size: 9,500 square feet
Number of sales staff: three
National delivery
Payment policy: One-third down as deposit payable by
cash, check, MasterCard, and Visa; balance due by
check or certified funds
Store manager: Leah Crawley

An extensive selection of Flexsteel.

Franklin Place (Level 3)
(828) 322-5539
Authorized dealer for Franklin Place, Pulaski, OID
Imports
Annual sales: February, July
Number of sales staff: one
Telephone orders accepted with payment in full
Payment Policy: Cash and checks accepted

Authentic reproductions of Early French furniture and
accents, including mantels, columns, bars, and sinks. There is
also an extensive collection of Indonesian teak garden furniture and unique accessories. Custom orders available.

Gallery of Lights (Level 3)
(828) 324-6337
(828) 327-9894 (fax)
gallery@abts.net
www.galleryoflights.com
Authorized dealer for dozens of lighting manufacturers
including Quoizel, Classic, Fine Art Lamps, Waterford,
Dale Tiffany, Meyda Tiffany

Annual sales: February
Established: 1986
Size: 2,000 square feet
Number of sales staff: two
Telephone/Internet orders are accepted
Payment policy: Payment in full at time of purchase;
    cash, check, Visa, and MasterCard accepted
Store manager: Tony Watts

The only store in the Mart that exclusively sells lighting.
You'll find chandeliers in crystal, alabaster, and wrought iron,
a wide range of lamps, and even a selection of accent furniture. If you need to illuminate your room or your home, this
is the place to do it. The staff is knowledgeable and they can
help you get the lighting that will work for you.

↣ **Henredon Factory Outlet** (Level 1)
(828) 322-7111
(828) 322-6839 (fax)
Authorized outlet for Henredon
Annual sales: January, February, May, November
Established: 1991
Size: 34,000 square feet
Number of sales staff: four
Telephone orders accepted
Payment policy: Payment in full upon purchase; cash,
    check, Visa, American Express, MasterCard
Store manager: Gary Liverman

Henredon is a full-line manufacturer that produces dining
room, bedroom, and occasional pieces in addition to sofas,
ottomans, chairs, loveseats, and sectionals. In the outlet you'll
find a mishmash of choices—constantly changing, never the
same stock twice—all well below the already discounted retail
prices of other local stores. What you'll find in this store (as

> *"When you're computing savings, remember that there's no such thing as a free lunch. Even if a store boasts free shipping, that cost is factored into the price of your furniture somewhere along the line. It doesn't mean that it isn't a good value, but don't be fooled into thinking that the shipping cost isn't factored in somewhere."* —STEVE MCNEELY, PRESIDENT, DONLAMOR, INC., RETAIL HOME FURNISHINGS

at most outlets) is showroom samples, slightly imperfect, and discontinued furniture. The tradeoff is that there are no custom orders from the store—what you see is what you get. You buy it as you see it and if it isn't on the floor, it's not available at the outlet price. What might have been here yesterday and isn't on the floor today is gone. It's hit or miss but when you hit expect to save *big*. The sales staff, unlike at many other outlets around the state, are as experienced as any you'll find anywhere else. Some even have education in decorating and interior design. Don't be afraid to ask lots of questions and consult on your purchasing plans. You'll be surprised by how helpful these salespeople are and they might be able to help you do some mixing and matching. Salesperson Eric Young is particularly helpful and conscientious.

⤛ **Hickory Park** (Levels 2 & 3, including The Leather Gallery and The Work Station on Level 2)
(828) 322-4440
(828) 322-4170 (fax)
www.hickorypark.com
Authorized dealer for more than 30 manufacturers including Kincaid, Rowe, Hekman, Kingsdown, Spring Air, Charleston Forge, Creative Ideas, C.R. Laine, Hammary, Dinaire, Leather Trend, Classic Leather
Annual Sales: February, May, July, November

Established: 1987, original store established in 1982
Size: 40,000 square feet
Number of sales staff: 24
Telephone orders accepted as per individual manufac-
    turer restrictions
National Delivery
Payment policy: One-third down as deposit payable by
    cash, check, MasterCard, and Visa; balance due by
    check or certified funds
Store manager: Brian Gee

One of the Mart's oldest tenants, this store really covers all
of the home furnishing bases. It is particularly strong on the
home office selections and has the Mart exclusive on Kincaid
furniture. Stock includes a large selection of solid wood—the
largest display in the Mart—casual dining, leather, bedding,
and executive home office furnishings. For convenience to the
shopper, Hickory Park displays like furniture together. So, for
example, you'll find all of the bar stools (the biggest display in
the Mart) in one place regardless of the manufacturer. There
is also a Hickory Park clearance center.

↦ **Hickory White/Theodore Alexander/Ferguson-
Copeland Factory Outlet** (Level 4)
(828) 327-3766
(828) 327-3104 (fax)
Authorized outlet for Hickory White, Theodore Alexan-
    der, Ferguson-Copland, and Carolina Tables of Hickory
Annual sales: January, May, November
Established: 2000
Size: 10,000 square feet
Number of sales staff: two
Payment policy: Payment in full upon purchase; cash,
    check, Visa, American Express, MasterCard
Store manager: Jeffrey Mingus

Part of the Theodore Alexander/Ferguson-Copeland outlet store, if you're in the market (or even if you're not) for furniture from these manufacturers this outlet store is the place to begin your hunt. Stock includes a continuously evolving selection of showroom samples, discontinued items, dealer returns, and slightly imperfect furniture. Don't be afraid to ask the salespeople lots of questions and consult with them on your purchasing plans. You'll be surprised by how helpful they are and they might be able to help you do some mixing and matching.

Hollin Gate Factory Outlet (Level 4)
(828) 324-2442

See Century listing, page 173, for details.

Hollin Gate Gallery (Level 4)
(828) 324-9400
www.hollingate.com
Authorized dealer for Howard Miller, Sligh Clocks,
    Colonial, J. Mallory Smythe, Distinction Leather
Annual sales: February, July
Established: 1985 in Mart, first store in 1974
Size: 11,000 square feet
Number of sales staff: three
Telephone orders accepted
Payment policy: Payment in full upon purchase of goods;
    cash, check, and bank card accepted

The Hollin Gate Gallery has a unique look of mixing new furniture with antiques, art, and bronzes. In addition to the manufacturers listed above, Hollin Gate also specializes in clocks, particularly grandfather clocks, plus curios and bronze statues. Custom orders available.

⇥ **Home Focus**
(828) 324-7742
(828) 327-3825 (fax)
Authorized dealer for Palliser, Highland House, Harrods, AICO, Butler, Serta, Kessler, Cramco, CMI, Schnadig, Hyundai
Annual sales: January, February, July, December
Established: 1986
Size: 22,000 square feet
Telephone orders are accepted as per individual manufacturer restrictions
Payment policy: Deposit at time of purchase, balance due before shipping; cash, check, Visa, MasterCard, Discover accepted
Store manager: Steve Noble

There's a lot to be said for a store that's one of the original tenants in the Mart. Not only has Home Focus been here since the beginning, but it also has the *original* Mart sales staff. Talk about longevity. Home Focus specializes in middle- to high-end products and everything is of superb quality: All wood frames, all eight-way hand-tied springs, global purchasing of leather in large volume (and the savings are passed on to the consumer). "Because of our volume purchasing, we can sell leather sofas at a fabric price," says manager Steve Noble. If you plan to make some big purchases, consider joining the "Home Focus membership club." For $25 you get an extra 10

> *"It's important to understand that you have to allot a considerable amount of time to shop here. Stopping "for a peek" on your way through town won't help you accomplish anything; you'll only leave frustrated."* —FRANK GARRIGA, OWNER, STUDIO 70 FURNITURE

percent off your entire purchase. Sale items are an extra 5 percent. The $25 membership earns itself back immediately.

House of Mirrors (Level 2)
(828) 323-8893
(828) 431-4765 (fax)
mirrors@hickory.net
Authorized dealer for Carvers' Guild, Arte De Mexico, Capel, Dauphine, Carolina Mirror, Uttermost, Sarreid LTD, Astoria, and Windsor Art
Annual sales: May, November after Market sales
Established: 1995
Size: 1,000 square feet
Sales staff: One full time, three part time (one with formal design education)
Telephone orders accepted
Payment policy: Payment due in full upon placement of order; check, Visa, MasterCard, and Discover accepted.

The name indicates the focus of the stock here, and House of Mirrors does specialize in mirrors (over 4,000 to choose from). But you'll also find slipcover furniture (another specialty of the house), iron furniture, rugs, hand-carved furnishings, and accessories. Probably the strongest selling point for House of Mirrors, though, is that it is the *only* store in the area that makes custom mirrors: any size up to 10 feet tall and 8 feet wide.

Intro Outlet
(828) 322-4426
(828) 322-4481 (fax)
introhickory@aol.com
www.introfurniture.com
Authorized dealer for Amisco, Dinec, Robin Bruce, Dellarobbia, Directional, Elite, Creative Elegance,

Pietrarte, Huppe, Melateck, Calligaris, Chairworks, Thayer Coggin

Annual sales: February, July (Mart-wide sales); offer a special almost every month and always have reduced price manufacturer samples

Established: 1999

Number of sales staff: three (two of the three Intro employees are also designers with design degrees)

Telephone/Internet orders are accepted

Payment policy: Deposit due at time of purchase, balance due before shipping; cash, check, American Express, Discover, MasterCard, and Visa accepted

Store manager: Ann Hooper

You can expect to find the lowest (always) discounted prices in this Intro Outlet. Intro has an eclectic mix of transitional and contemporary furniture, handcrafted contemporary pieces, and accessories. It is the first contemporary outlet in the Mart. Don't be afraid to ask the staff for help. They're friendly and experienced in sales and design.

Ironstone Galleries (Level 2)

(828) 304-1094

(828) 304-1095 (fax)

ironstone@abts.net

Authorized dealer for Parlance, Michael Thomas, Legacy Leather, A.R.A. Furniture, J. Royal, Royale Komfort, Murray Feiss, Frederick Cooper, Engelite

Annual sales: July, February

Established: 1997

Size: 9,000 square feet

Number of sales staff: two

Telephone orders accepted if customer has visited the store previously

Payment policy: Deposit due at time of purchase, balance due before shipping; cash, check, Discover, MasterCard, and Visa accepted
Store manager: Gary Lambert

Ironstone has the exclusive in the region on Parlance furniture and the value to you is great because of the factory-direct savings. The original line of transitional furniture at Ironstone is ideal for a distinctive look: Furnishings often include a blend of metal, glass, stone, or marble. Customized furniture is not only available but also encouraged. And it is widely known within the Mart that the selection of parson's chairs is hard to beat.

La Petite France (Level 2)
(828) 326-9030
(828) 326-9030 (fax)
www.mariefrancefurniture.com
Annual sales: February, May, November
Established: 1998
Size: 800 square feet
Number of sales staff: three
Telephone orders accepted with deposit
National delivery
Payment policy: Deposit due at time of purchase, balance due before shipping; cash, check, American Express, Discover, MasterCard, and Visa accepted

Walking into La Petite France is like stepping back in time. All of the solid wood (in cherry, oak, and beech) furniture is made in France and each piece is an historical reproduction. The finishes are unique to La Petite France and the furniture comes direct from the manufacturer—which translates into savings for you.

➤➤ **La-Z-Boy by Hickory Park** (Level 3)
(828) 326-4440, general number
(828) 322-7275, Generations gallery
Authorized dealer for La-Z-Boy
National delivery
Payment policy: One-third down as deposit payable by
cash, check, MasterCard, and Visa; balance due by
check or certified funds

Adjoining the Comfort Zone, the La-Z-Boy Gallery has a selection of recliners, incliners, sleepers, and generally relaxation-inducing furniture that's not to be believed. Sit down and take a load off in one of the dozens of nap-appropriate furnishings that have come to be known as America's favorite recliners. And not to be missed for furnishing children's rooms is the Generations gallery by La-Z-Boy, perhaps the best children's furnishing selection in the Mart, where, by the way, there is a comfortable kids' room set up complete with a television and videos.

Lexington/Drexel Heritage Galleries by Boyles
(Level 2)
(828) 326-1060
(828) 326-1097 (fax)
store11@boyles.com
Authorized dealer for Drexel Heritage, Lexington Furni-
ture Brands, Bob Timberlake, Fine Art, Howard
Miller, Kingsdown, Palmer Home Collection,
Maitland-Smith, Lillian August, Ziba Rugs and many
others
Annual sales: February
Established: 1993
Size: 20,000 square feet
Number of sales staff: nine (one with formal design
education)

Telephone/Internet sales are accepted per individual
    manufacturer restrictions
Delivery: National delivery with Classic Moving and
    Storage
Payment policy: One-third down as deposit by check,
    MasterCard, or Visa; balance due in certified funds
    upon delivery
Store manager: Angie Winkler

See Boyles Galleries, page 170, for details.

Nostalgia Handcrafted Furniture (Level 1)
(828) 325-4800
(828) 325-4805 (fax)
nostalgia@twave.net
www.nostalgiafurniture.com
Authorized dealer for, amongst others, Nostalgia,
    Meyda, Sagefield Leather, and Vineyard Furniture
Annual sales: March
Established: 1990
Size: 10,000 square feet
Number of sales staff: two (one with formal design
    education)
Telephone/Internet orders accepted
Nationwide delivery
Payment policy: Cash, MasterCard, and Visa accepted
Store manager: Charles Sparks

The traditional handcrafted furniture you see in Nostalgia
is the sort you expect to be handed down from one generation
to the next. Nostalgia determines the process of the furniture
from start—beginning with selection of the wood—to finish
with the manufacturing, carving, the finish, and distribution
to you. There are several reproduction antique lines made
from Indonesian and South American mahogany as well as a

Country French line made in pine. Garden and indoor furniture is made from Indonesian teak.

Pennsylvania House (Level 4)
(828) 261-2026
(828) 261-2049 (fax)
Authorized dealer for Pennsylvania House, Surrey Limited, Emerson Et Cie, Cotswold, Serta Mattress Company, and many others
Annual sales: First weekend of May and November
Established: 1999
Size: 10,000 square feet
Number of sales staff: five
Telephone orders accepted—confirmed in writing via fax
Payment policy: Deposit due at time of purchase, balance due before shipping; cash, check, MasterCard, and Visa accepted
Store manager: Lynn Scott

Pennsylvania House at the Mart is the largest area showroom for Pennsylvania House furnishings. And that's only the beginning: There are plenty of other manufacturers to choose from and the sales staff will make you feel at ease while you shop this welcoming showroom. Custom orders available.

Reflections Furniture (Level 3)
(828) 327-8485
(828) 327-8316 (fax)
reflections@twave.net
www.reflectionsfurniture.com
Authorized dealer for Natuzzi, Ekornes, American Leather, Trica, John Charles Designs, Lazar, Shermag, Ello, Visu, Axi, Elite, Gamma, Stone International, Elite Tables
Annual sales: February, May, July, and November

Established: 1989
Size: 5,000 square feet and growing
Number of sales staff: three
Telephone/Internet sales accepted as per manufacturer
    restrictions
In-home delivery/installation available
Payment policy: 50 percent down as deposit, balance due
    before shipping; MasterCard, Visa, Discover, cash,
    and personal checks accepted
Store manager: Beth Fonnesu

A family owned business, the specialty here is leather. The emphasis is on contemporary furnishings and unique accessories but there is also a selection of transitional and traditional furnishings (upholstery, tables, lamps, rugs, entertainment, dining) to round out the mix. One of three stores that this Belgian immigrant family owns. They started with a mere 1,000 feet and have grown to 20,000 in total. Custom orders available.

Resource Design (Level 3)
(828) 322-3161
(828) 322-3162
www.resourcedsgn.com
Annual sales: February, July
Established: 1990
Number of sales staff: four (all with formal design
    education)
Payment policy: Deposit due upon purchase, balance due
    before shipping; Visa, MasterCard, American Express,
    cash, and checks accepted
Store manager: Taria Stearns

Specializing in fabric, wallpaper, decorative trims, and drapery hardware. You don't have to worry that the staff here isn't design savvy because *all* of them have formal education in design. Custom bedding and window treatments are a specialty of the house.

⇥ **Robert Bergelin Company** (Level 3)
(828) 345-1500
(828) 345-0203 (fax)
www.rbcfurn.com
Robert Bergelin furniture
Established: 1993
Size: 4,000 square feet
Number of sales staff: five
Telephone orders accepted
Nationwide shipping with in-home installation
Payment policy: 50 percent down as deposit, balance due
    before shipping; cash and checks accepted
Store manager: Lynn Russell

See the entry for the Atrium Furniture Mall, High Point, for details.

Rug Room, The
(828) 324-1776
(828) 324-1676 (fax)
donlamor@twave.net
www.donlamor.com
Authorized dealer for Masterlooms, Feizy, Lotfy,
    M.E.R., Shalom Brothers, Samad Brothers, Obeetee,
    Nourison
Annual sales: February, May, August, November
Established: 1987
Size: 9,000 square feet
Number of sales staff: two
Telephone/Internet orders accepted
National delivery

Payment policy: Cash, check, Visa, and MasterCard are
    accepted
Store manager: Steve McNeely

You'll find a vast selection of rugs, both in the hanging
gallery and on the floor, in countless styles, colors, and
designs. Allow the sales staff to help you make the jump from
matching your room to your favorite rug to your furniture.

Sity Slicker (Level 2)
(828) 325-0092
(828) 325-0969 (fax)
www.sityslicker.com
Authorized dealer for Paul Robert, El Paso, William
    Sheppee, Pangaea Collection, Old Java, Natural
    Light, Montaage, Country Originals, Ozark Rustic
Annual sales: May, November
Established: 1995
Size: 2,500 square feet
Number of sales staff: three (one with formal design
    training)
Payment policy: 50 percent down as deposit; cash,
    checks, Visa, MasterCard, and Discover
Store manager: Jay R. Bunton

The overwhelming style selection at Sity Slicker is "cabin to
cottage." You won't find "fancy formal" furnishings here. Sity
Slicker primarily caters to people who are furnishing second
homes—often beach or lake homes—with casual furnishings.
But don't feel left out if you're furnishing your one and only:
This look is also great for a rustic den or guest room.

Southern Designs (Level 3)
(828) 328-8855
(828) 328-1806 (fax)

Authorized dealer for more than 30 furniture and accessory manufacturers including Athol, Brown Street, Chatham Furniture Reproductions, Hitchcock, Huntington House, Key City, Mobel, Richardson Brothers, Canal Dovre, Villageois

Annual sales: After Market sales; May, November

Established: 1987

Size: 14,000 square feet

Number of sales staff: four (one with formal design education)

Telephone sales accepted as per manufacturer restrictions

Payment policy: Deposit due upon purchase, balance due before shipping; checks, cash, and debit cards accepted

Southern Designs is a special operation in that the store is *employee* owned—always a good indication that the service will be top-notch and that every employee you deal with will be a professional (after all, it's their store's reputation on the line). The specialty here is solid wood, American-made furniture and 10-way hand-tied upholstered furniture in American Country, Shaker, and traditional styles.

Southern Style (Level 4)

(828) 322-7000

(828) 322-7220 (fax)

Authorized dealer for Southern of Conover and Presidential

Annual sales: January, February

Established: 2001, parent company established in 1884

Size: 8,400 square feet

Number of sales staff: two

Telephone orders are accepted

Payment policy: Deposit due at time of purchase, balance due before shipping; cash and checks accepted
Store manager: Rita Sims

Factory-direct store for Southern Furniture.

Theodore Alexander/Hickory White/Ferguson-Copeland Factory Outlet (Level 4)
(828) 327-3766

See listing under Hickory White Factory Outlet for details.

Thomasville Gallery by Boyles (Level 4)
(828) 326-1740
(828) 326-8766 (fax)
Authorized dealer for Thomasville Furniture Industries, Fine Art, Howard Miller, John Richard, Kingsdown, Ziba Rugs; other manufacturers available by catalog
Annual sales: May, November
Established: 1998
Size: 11,000 square feet
Number of sales staff: six
Telephone orders are accepted as per individual manufacturer restrictions
National delivery by Classic Moving and Storage, exclusively available to Boyles customers
Payment policy: One-third down as deposit by check, MasterCard, or Visa; balance due in certified funds upon delivery
Store manager: Judy Anders

This is one of four Boyles stores in the Mart (totaling more than 100,000 square feet) and the Mart's exclusive Thomasville dealer.

Timeless Interiors (Level 3)
(828) 325-0565
Authorized dealer for Hickory Hill, Elden, Hammer
Annual sales: May, November
Established: 1997
Size: 2,000 square feet
Number of sales staff: three (all with formal design
    education)
National delivery
Payment policy: Cash, checks, MasterCard, Visa

One-on-one design help is readily available in this relatively small and homey store. Don't be afraid to ask questions,
bring out the floor plans, and take advantage of the expert
sales staff.

The Wild Pear (Level 4)
(828) 326-9296
(828) 326-9332 (fax)
thewildpear@earthlink.net
Authorized dealer for Shabby Chic, Eminence
Annual sales: February, July
Established: 2000
Size: 400 square feet
Number of sales staff: four
Payment policy: Accept Visa, MasterCard, American Ex-
    press, cash, and checks; payment in full on special or-
    ders, 65 percent down on furniture and bedding orders

This store may be small but don't let that scare you away.
The selection includes upholstered furnishings (which have a
lifetime guarantee on the frame and seating), refurbished
antiques, and accessories. The staff is at the ready to help in
any way they can including working from your swatches to
putting a selection of bedding together for you while you shop.

Zagaroli Classics Fine Leather Furniture (Level 3)
(828) 328-3373
(828) 328-5839 (fax)
zagaroli@twave.net
www.zagarolileather.com
Authorized dealer for Zagaroli, Ardley Hall, Sweet
    Dreams, and Fabrice de Vilteneuve
Annual sales: February, May, July, November
Established: 1993
Size: 5,300 square feet
Number of sales staff: four (two with formal education in
    interior design)
Telephone orders accepted
Payment policy: 50 percent down as deposit, balance due
    before shipping; cash, check, MasterCard, Visa, Dis-
    cover, and American Express accepted
Store manager: Carol Furnas

Zagaroli features top-quality, bench-made leather furniture, all produced in Hickory. As a manufacturer, Zagaroli
Classics sells to dealers and designers across the country but
this store is the only place where the products are sold directly
to the consumer. Purchases from the store can be from stock
styles and designs, or custom. The attention to detail and
added personal touch is unique: Each order that goes through

*"If you want your leather or case goods to be perfect, you're
better off with a synthetic likeness because both materials are
natural—wood comes from trees and leather comes from animals—so there will be slight imperfections. Your skin isn't ex-
actly consistent over your entire body; it's the same with cows
and trees."* —STEVE NOBLE, GENERAL MANAGER AND VETERAN
SALESMAN, HOME FOCUS FURNITURE

the factory is identified by the customer's name, not by a production or style number. The showroom also offers gifts, accessories, case goods, and antiques.

CATAWBA FURNITURE MALL

377 Highway 70 S.W.; I-40 Exit 123
(800) 789-0686, (828) 324-9701
www.catawbafurniture.com
Hours: 10:00 AM–7:00 PM Monday–Saturday, Sunday
1:00 PM–5:00 PM (select galleries); closed January 1,
Easter, July 4, Thanksgiving, December 25

➻ **About Last Nite**
(828) 324-2830
(828) 324-2866 (fax)
Authorized linens dealer for Sferra, Peacock Alley, J.
Clayton International, Bella Notte, Fleur de Lis,
Home Treasures, Legacy, Matteo, Christian Aubry,
Austin Horn, Fino Lino, Koko, Christy, Wildcat,
Paper White, Sweet Dreams, Eastern Accents, Mystic
Valley Traders, Lucia, Designs, Banana Fish; also
carry furniture manufacturers Stone County, Old Bis-
cayne Designs, Excavo, Stylecraft of Thomasville
Annual sales: January white sale, after-Market sale in
May, after-Market sale in late October/early
November
Established: December 1999
Size: 6,000 square feet
Number of sales staff: four (one with formal design
education)
National delivery in the continental U.S., also combine
to ship with other retailers in the area
Telephone/Internet sales are accepted

Payment policy: 50 percent due on deposit, remainder
due at shipping; all major credit cards are accepted
Store Manager: Regina Garriga

See the entry for About Last Nite in The Atrium, High
Point. At this larger store, you have all the same amazingly
soft and gorgeous White-House-worthy linens, and also don't
forget about bringing up baby: About Last Nite has baby
beds, changing tables, armoires, gliders and, of course, linens.
Snuggly blankets, soft chenilles, velvets, quilts, baby-soft
throws and towels, and complete baby bed ensembles including bumpers, skirts, sheets, blankets, pillows, and duvets to
round out the selection.

American Décor
(828) 322-4534
(828) 322-2662 (fax)
www.catawbafurniture.com
Authorized dealer for dozens of manufacturers including
American Drew, Clayton Marcus, Hurtado, King
Hickory, J. Royale, Cochrane, Craftmaster, Virginia
House, Barcalounger, Bassett
Annual sales: April, October, and during mall sales and
festivals
Established: 1999
Size: 40,000 square feet
Number of sales staff: six (three with formal design
education)
Telephone/Internet orders accepted
National delivery
Payment policy: Visa, MasterCard, debit card, Dis-
cover, personal checks, and cash accepted; financing
is available
Store manager: Mary Messines

You'll feel at home as you wander through the galleries at American Décor: From room to room, it's an endless cornucopia of furnishing options. Especially strong in manufacturers American Drew and Clayton Marcus, that's only the tip of the iceberg. All of the "rooms" are accessorized and the selection of juvenile and youth furniture is especially strong.

American Oak & Cherry
(828) 324-5055 (phone and fax)
Annual sales: After-Market sales, spring and autumn
Established: 1996
Size: 18,000 square feet
Number of sales staff: three (two with formal design
    education)

A custom oak and cherry store, everything here is solid wood. You'll find no particle board and no veneers. Especially strong in dining room and bedroom sets, don't overlook the home-office selections, too.

Ashley Furniture HomeStore
(828) 304-0741
(828) 304-0841 (fax)
Hours: 10:00 AM–7:00 PM Monday–Friday, 9:00 AM–7:00
    PM Saturday, 1:00 PM–5:00 PM Sunday; closed major
    holidays
Authorized dealer for several manufacturers including
    Ashley Furniture and Millennium
Established: 1999
Size: 54,000 square feet
Number of sales staff: eight (one with formal design
    education)
Telephone orders accepted
International delivery

Payment policy: 50 percent down as deposit, balance due
before shipping; cash, checks, and all credit cards are
accepted

Store manager: Crystal Hutson

When you step into the heart of the Ashley store, you
immediately feel at home: There are complimentary fresh
baked cookies by the main counter, a Men's Club Room with
a big-screen TV for exhausted shoppers, the Kid's Rooms
with cartoon videos for children, and coffee to keep you
pumping. And that's pretty much the attitude around here:
The staff wants you to feel comfortable and at ease, and
because it's the largest Ashley Furniture HomeStore in the
world you'll find no shortage of what you're looking for.

Broyhill Showcase Gallery

(828) 261-7240

(828) 327-4159 (fax)

Hours: 9:00 AM–7:00 PM Monday–Saturday, Sunday 1:00
PM–5:00 PM; closed major holidays

Authorized dealer for Broyhill

Annual sales: After Market, May and November

Established: March, 2001

Size: 40,000 square feet

Number of sales staff: four (one with formal design
training)

Telephone/Internet orders accepted

National delivery

Payment policy: 50 percent down as deposit with check,
cash, money order, or Discover; balance payable with
any of above and MasterCard or Visa

Store manager: Kay Hefner

The largest Broyhill gallery in the world, you'll not only
have the vast selection but also countless custom options.

Cornerstone Wine & Gifts

(828) 324-9701 ext. 106

(828) 324-5848

wineshop@catawbafurniture.com

www.catawbafurniture.com

Hours: 9:00 AM–6:00 PM Monday–Friday, 10:00 AM–6:00 PM Saturday; closed Sunday and major holidays

Established: February 2001

Size: 7,500 square feet

Number of sales staff: four (one with formal design education)

Telephone/Internet sales accepted

Payment policy: Payment in full at time of purchase; cash, checks, Visa, MasterCard, and traveler's checks accepted

Store manager: David Garriga

The largest wine store in the area, that's not all Cornerstone has to recommend it. Pick up those accent furniture items for your home—unique wine racks, plush leather chairs—or stop in for a bottle of regional N.C. wine (and other international favorites) or a made-to-order gift basket. You'll find all of your wine needs served up here, from wine glasses to corkscrews to gourmet snacks.

Eclectic Solutions by Blowing Rock Furniture

(828) 267-0313, (828) 322-4534 ext. 2011

(828) 322-2662

www.blowingrockfurniture.com

Hours: 9:00 AM–7:00 PM Monday–Saturday, 1:00 PM–5:00 PM Sunday; closed major holidays

Authorized dealer for Hurtado, J. Royale, King Hickory, and others

Annual sales: May, October

Established: 1998

Size: 35,000 square feet

Number of sales staff: three (two with formal design
   education)

Telephone orders accepted payable by debit and Discover cards

National delivery

Payment policy: 50 percent down as deposit with check,
   cash, money order, or Discover; balance payable with
   any of above and MasterCard or Visa

Store manager: Kimlie Fox

Originally conceived of as a service for interior designers,
Eclectic Solutions has evolved into a full-service, off-the-
floor, and custom order store. Specialties include unique and
higher-end furnishings.

Lifestyles
(828) 324-9701
(828) 322-4947 (fax)
www.blowingrockfurniture.com
Hours: 9:00 AM–7:00 PM Monday–Saturday, 1:00
   PM–5:00 PM Sunday; closed major holidays
Authorized dealer for Klaussner including Sealy and
   Dick Idol
Annual sales: May, November
Established: 1999
Size: More than 32,000 square feet
Number of sales staff: three
Telephone orders accepted
National delivery
Payment policy: 50 percent down as deposit with check,
   cash, money order, or Discover; balance payable with
   any of above and MasterCard or Visa
Store manager: Stefani Beane

This store speaks for itself. The selection of Sealy furniture is extensive and the prices are remarkable. The staff is friendly and many have a background in furniture manufacturing. If you're into the rustic look, be sure to check out the new Dick Idol Gallery.

⇥ **Studio 70**
(828) 322-2800
(828) 322-2026
www.studioseventy.com
Authorized dealer for Carter, Carson's Weiman, Hulsta, Calligaris, Hjellegjerde, Rossetto, Tempur-Pedic, Palecek, Cebu
Annual sales: May, October
Established: January 2000
Size: 16,000 square feet
Number of sales staff: two
Telephone orders accepted
National delivery
Payment policy: 50 percent down as deposit, balance due before shipping; forms of payment accepted: Master-Card, Visa, Discover, American Express, and personal check
Store manager: Frank Garriga

I must admit, I'm not a big fan of contemporary furniture, or so I thought before I walked into Studio 70. The selection of contemporary furniture is the largest of any store in Hickory and I was surprised by how many of the pieces I not only liked for their whimsical nature but also for their simplicity and practicality. Many of the furnishings can be upholstered in white or beige, or, if you're really looking to make a statement, red or purple. There is also a great selection of accessories: Lights, fountains, mobiles, and an annex of rattan

Contemporary furniture is often a comfortable,

tasteful,

and creative alternative to traditional designs.

furniture. Even if you're not a "contemporary person" it's worth a peek if only to see the versatility of the contemporary look.

HICKORY TO LENOIR (ROUTE 321—22 MILES OF FURNITURE)

Many of the customers who strike out along Route 321 are regional regulars who are familiar with the different stores, bargain hunters checking the outlets, and shoppers who are looking for a lower-end selection (i.e., lower prices per piece). As one local confided: "The only reason you wouldn't find what you were looking for in the Mart would be that the price point was too high. I'd direct that person to Route 321, where there's a selection with a lower price tag."

Blowing Rock Furniture
(828) 396-3186
(828) 396-6031
furnitureinfo@blowingrockfurniture.com
www.blowingrockfurniture.com
Hours: 9:00 AM–6:00 PM Monday–Saturday; closed Sunday and major holidays
Authorized dealer for dozens of manufacturers including Thomasville, Broyhill, Stanley, Klaussner, Bob Timberlake, Universal, American Drew, and Serta
Annual sales: February, May, October
Established: 1978
Size: 82,000 square feet
Number of sales staff: nine
Telephone/Internet orders accepted as per individual manufacturer restrictions
National delivery
Payment policy: 50 percent down as deposit payable in

cash, check, MasterCard, Visa, and Discover; balance
due in certified funds; financing available
Store manager: Amy Gowings

The furniture at Blowing Rock is ideal for people looking to
spend less on furniture. The store is set up in completely accessorized galleries giving the "in-home" feel to the showrooms.
A special Dick Idol gallery, the largest in the area, features rustic, country furniture. While this store offers great value on
well-known manufacturer brands, it is important to note that
as of the writing of this book Blowing Rock had an unsatisfactory rating with the Better Business Bureau. In all fairness,
with the volume of orders that Blowing Rock (and all of the
furniture stores in North Carolina, for that matter) handles
there are always bound to be unsatisfied customers; however,
an unsatisfactory rating is not to be taken lightly, so please
check in with the BBB before making any commitments.

Bonita
210 13th Street S.W. (off Route 321)
Hickory
(828) 432-1992
(828) 324-7972
www.bonitafurniture.com
Hours: 9:00 AM–5:00 PM Monday–Saturday; closed Sunday and major holidays
Authorized dealer for dozens of manufacturers including
American Drew, Barcalounger, Bernhardt, Clayton
Marcus, Hooker, Lane, La-Z-Boy, Leathercraft, Lexington, Pennsylvania House, Serta Bedding, Stanley
Thomasville, Wesley Allen
Payment policy: 50 percent down as deposit, balance due
before shipping; cash, checks, Visa, and MasterCard ac-
cepted
National shipping and in-home set-up available

When you mention Route 321, Bonita is usually the first name out of people's mouths. A large store with a large selection, Bonita has a longstanding reputation and an experienced sales staff. If it's a room, an office or a house you need to furnish, you'll find everything you need, from furniture to accessories.

Boyles Clearance Center

739 Old Lenoir Road
(828) 326-1700
Hours: 9:00 AM–6:00 PM Monday–Friday, 9:00 AM–5:00
    PM Saturday; closed Sunday and major holidays
Established: 1997
Size: 18,000 square feet
National shipping
Payment policy: Payment in full at time of purchase;
    payable by cash, check, MasterCard, and Visa

The Boyles clearance center is on the same site as the original Boyles "Country Shop." There is still a retail store adjacent to the clearance center, though it is quite small in comparison with the new Boyles showrooms in High Point and the Hickory Furniture Mart. The Boyles clearance center, like with the outlets, offers discounts on discontinued items, scratch and dent, Market samples, and closeouts. You'll find no glamorous showroom setups here—it's all warehouse-

---

"Find a salesperson you like and let them help and guide you. They will help you make sense of it all—narrow down the field and explain the ropes. Even if you don't buy from that salesperson, they can still point you in the right direction."
—TIM SHEPARD, CAREER SALESMAN (MORE THAN 25 YEARS), ROSE FURNITURE COMPANY

style display (in fact, the clearance center is in the old ware-house)—but there's lots of furniture to look through and the savings can be great.

↦ **Thomasville Furniture Factory Outlet**
  3064 Hickory Boulevard (Route 321)
  (828) 728-4108
  Authorized outlet for Thomasville, Hickory Chair,
    Highland House, and Pearson
  Payment in full at time of purchase; cash, checks, and
    credit cards accepted; shipping available

Of the Thomasville outlets, this is my *favorite* location. The space is large and open, the staff is courteous and helpful.

See High Point listings for other Thomasville outlet locations.

LENOIR MALL—MANUFACTURER OUTLETS

  1031 Morganton Boulevard S.W. (Highway 18)
  (828) 757-2780

There are four manufacturer outlets in the Lenoir Mall: Bernhardt, Kincaid, and two Broyhill stores. And if you're interested in these manufacturers it's certainly worth a look. Here, as with all outlets, it's hit or miss, no returns, and what you see is what you get. But when you do hit, you'll likely be saving big off the manufacturer's suggested retail price. Stock includes closeouts, Market samples, and one-of-a-kind pieces.

  Bernhardt Furniture Outlet
  (828) 758-0532
  www.bernhardtfurniture.com
  9:00 AM–6:00 PM Monday–Saturday, 1:00 PM–5:00 PM
    Sunday; closed major holidays

Established: 1996
Size: 25,000 square feet
National shipping
Payment policy: Payable in full at time of purchase; cash, check, Visa, MasterCard, and Discover accepted

Broyhill Outlet
(828) 758-8899
Hours: 10:00 AM–6:00 PM Monday, Wednesday, Friday, and Saturday; 10:00 AM–7:00 PM Tuesday and Thursday; 1:00 PM–5:00 PM Sunday; closed major holidays
Size: 15,000 (since 1997) and 10,000 square feet (since 1999)
National shipping
Payment policy: Payment in full at time of purchase; payable by cash, check, MasterCard, and Visa

Kincaid Outlet
(828) 754-2126
Hours: 9:00 AM–6:00 PM Monday–Saturday, 1:00 PM–5:00 PM Sunday; closed major holidays
Established: 1997
Size: 18,000 square feet
National shipping
Payment in full at time of purchase; payable by cash, check, MasterCard, and Visa

ACCOMMODATIONS

Hickory has an abundance of clean, modern, well-priced hotels. The two that stand out, indicated by an ➵, are on the premises of or extremely close to (with a free shuttle service) the large furniture malls—which makes life that much simpler.

Comfort Suites
1125 13th Avenue Drive S.E.
Hickory, NC 28602
(828) 323-1211
(828) 322-4395 (fax)
www.hgmhotels.com
116 Suites
Nonsmoking rooms, outdoor pool, handicapped accessible rooms, TV/cable, health club, dry cleaning/laundry service available weekdays, guest laundry, complimentary full buffet breakfast, manager's reception Monday–Thursday, refrigerator, microwave, coffeemaker, wet bar, sleeper sofa, complimentary *USA Today* newspaper, whirlpool rooms, meeting rooms available

Courtyard by Marriott
1946 13th Avenue Drive S.E.
Hickory, NC 28602
(828) 267-2100
(828) 324-2461 (fax)
www.courtyard.com
140 Rooms; 6 Suites
Nonsmoking rooms, handicapped accessible rooms, indoor pool, Jacuzzi, guest laundry, same-day dry cleaning available Monday–Friday, exercise room, 24-hour grab-and-go food pantry, restaurant open for breakfast, microwave and refrigerator in some rooms, cable/satellite TV, complimentary newspaper, data ports, hairdryer, coffeemaker, iron/ironing board, two-line phones, voice mail, meeting rooms available, business center, furniture shoppers package

Days Inn
1710 Fairgrove Church Road
Conover, NC 28613

(828) 465-2378
(828) 465-6488 (fax)
www.hgmhotels.com
59 Rooms
Nonsmoking rooms, kitchenette, outdoor pool, handicapped accessible rooms, TV/cable, exercise room, guest laundry, complimentary continental breakfast, data ports, minisuites have microwave, fridge, coffeepots, hairdryers, VCRs, vending, complimentary *USA Today* newspaper, free local calls, meeting rooms available

Fairfield Inn
1950 13th Avenue Drive S.E.
Hickory, NC 28602
(828) 431-3000
(828) 431-4714 (fax)
www.fairfieldinnhickory.com
108 Rooms
Nonsmoking rooms, heated indoor pool, health club, handicapped accessible rooms, TV/cable, guest laundry, complimentary continental breakfast, free local calls, outdoor patio near pool, vending, data ports, six executive king rooms with microwave and refrigerator, meeting rooms available, adjacent to Hickory Metro Convention Center, furniture shoppers rates

"You'll want to be open-minded when you come here because, though you should do your homework and have an idea of what you want before you come (narrow down styles and colors), you'll see things here that you won't see at home—there's just that much to choose from." —RON STEVENS, VICE PRESIDENT OF SALES & MARKETING, HIGH POINT CONVENTION AND VISITORS BUREAU

Halle House
25 Hillside Avenue
Granite Falls, NC 28630
(828) 313-3989
(828) 313-0148 (fax)
www.hallehouse.com
Three Rooms
Nonsmoking rooms, business center, 3.5 acres of land-
scaped grounds, complimentary full breakfast, afternoon refreshments

Hampton Inn
1520 13th Avenue Drive S.E.
Hickory, NC 28602
(828) 323-1150
(828) 324-8979 (fax)
www.hampton-inn.com
119 Rooms
Nonsmoking rooms, outdoor pool, handicapped accessible rooms, TV/cable, health club nearby, complimentary deluxe continental breakfast, hairdryers in some
rooms, free local calls, 250-channel TV/free
HBO/pay-per-view, data ports, free *USA Today* newspaper, coffee/fruit 24 hours, meeting rooms available,
furniture shoppers rates

Hickory Bed & Breakfast
464 7th Street S.W.
Hickory, NC 28602
(800) 654-2961; (828) 324-0548
(828) 324-7434 (fax)
www.hickorybedandbreakfast.com
Four Rooms
Outdoor pool, TV/cable, includes full breakfast, business
center

Hickory Motor Lodge
484 Highway 70 S.W.
Hickory, NC 28602
(828) 322-1740
(828) 322-6824 (fax)
86 Rooms
Nonsmoking rooms, guest laundry, complimentary
morning coffee in lobby, free cable/HBO, some data
ports

➻ **Holiday Inn Express**
2250 Highway 70 S.E.
Hickory, NC 28602
(828) 328-2081
(828) 328-2085 (fax)
www.basshotels.com
60 Rooms; 2 two-bedroom suites; 2 efficiency units
w/kitchenettes
Nonsmoking rooms, handicapped accessible rooms,
TV/cable, extensive health club, pets allowed, dry
cleaning/laundry service available weekdays, complimentary deluxe continental breakfast, free local calls,
free *USA Today* newspaper Monday–Friday, racquet-
ball, movie channel, data ports, meeting rooms available, adjacent to Hickory Furniture Mart, furniture
shoppers rates

On the premises of the Hickory Furniture Mart, this is the
obvious and simple choice if you're shopping at the Mart.
Having your hotel right there makes it easy to take breaks,
check on the family, and otherwise secure some of the com-
forts of home during your shopping marathon. Rooms are
spacious and clean.

Holiday Inn Express
104 10th Street N.W.
Conover, NC 28613
(800) 710-9110; (828) 465-7070
(828) 465-7090 (fax)
www.basshotels.com
92 Rooms; 26 Suites
Nonsmoking rooms, outdoor pool, fitness room, handicapped accessible rooms, TV/cable/HBO, dry cleaning/laundry service available weekdays, guest laundry, complimentary breakfast, in-room coffee, iron and ironing boards in room, free *USA Today* newspaper Monday–Friday, in-room movies available, full two-room kitchen suites, meeting rooms available

Holiday Inn Select
1385 Lenoir-Rhyne Blvd. S.E.
Hickory, NC 28602
(828) 323-1000
(828) 322-4275 (fax)
200 Rooms, 4 Suites
www.holidayinnselecthickory.com
Nonsmoking rooms, restaurant, bar/lounge, room service, indoor pool, health club, handicap rooms, TV/cable, dry cleaning/laundry service available weekdays, guest laundry, complimentary morning coffee, tea, weekday newspaper, salon adjacent, data ports, iron and ironing boards, in-room coffee, executive wing with club room serving continental breakfast and afternoon hors d'oeuvres, furniture shoppers packages, meeting rooms available

Howard Johnson Inn
483 Highway 70 S.W.
Hickory, NC 28602

(828) 322-1600
(828) 327-2041 (fax)
64 Rooms
Nonsmoking rooms, restaurant, bar/lounge, outdoor
pool, health club, handicap rooms, TV/cable, dry
cleaning/laundry service available weekdays, guest
laundry, complimentary in-room coffee, complimentary *USA Today* newspaper Monday–Friday, data
ports, Friday-night seafood buffet, Sunday lunch buffet, meeting rooms available

Jameson Inn
1120 13th Avenue Drive S.E.
Hickory, NC 28602
(828) 304-0410
(828) 304-0411 (fax)
www.jamesoninns.com
59 Rooms
Nonsmoking rooms, outdoor pool, fitness room, handicapped accessible rooms, TV/cable, complimentary
breakfast, complimentary *USA Today* newspaper Monday–Friday, two- and three-room suites available, premium rooms with coffeepot, microwave, fridge, and
recliner, data ports, all exterior entrances, hairdryers,
iron and boards available

➻ **Park Inn Gateway Conference Center**
909 Highway 70 S.W.
Hickory, NC 28602
(828) 328-5101; (800) 789-0686
(828) 328-8943 (fax)
www.gateway-hotel.com
109 Rooms; 9 Suites
Nonsmoking rooms, outdoor pool, handicapped accessible rooms, TV/cable, laundry/dry cleaning service,

complimentary deluxe continental breakfast buffet daily, free *USA Today* newspaper, free local calls, hairdryers, coffee- and teamakers, in-room voice mail, data ports, airport transportation available, executive suites, meeting rooms available

This is the most comfortable of the major Hickory hotels, and is adjacent to the Catawba Furniture Mall. Service is particularly friendly and the rooms are in tip-top shape with all modern amenities.

Quality Inn & Suites
1725 13th Avenue Drive N.W.
Hickory, NC 28601
(828) 431-2100
(828) 431-2109 (fax)
www.hgmhotels.com
100 Rooms; 40 Suites
Nonsmoking rooms, outdoor pool, health club, handicapped accessible rooms, TV/cable, guest laundry, dry cleaning/laundry service available Monday–Friday, complimentary full buffet breakfast, complimentary manager's cocktails Monday–Thursday, airport shuttle, data ports, suites with whirlpools, microwave, in-room coffee, refrigerators, and speaker phones, meeting rooms available

Ramada Inn
1607 Fairgrove Church Road
Conover, NC 28613
(828) 465-1100
(828) 465-3090 (fax)
www.hgmhotels.com
155 Rooms

Nonsmoking rooms, restaurant, indoor and outdoor
pools, health club, TV/cable, dry cleaning/laundry
service available weekdays, guest laundry, complimentary continental breakfast, complimentary *USA Today*
newspaper Monday–Friday, executive floor, data
ports, meeting rooms available

Red Roof Inn
1184 Lenoir-Rhyne Blvd.
Hickory, NC 28602
(828) 323-1500
(828) 323-1509 (fax)
108 Rooms
Nonsmoking rooms, handicap rooms, pets allowed,
TV/satellite, complimentary coffee in lobby, complimentary *USA Today* newspaper, pay-per-view and
Nintendo, business king rooms available, data ports,
microwaves/refrigerators available, free local calls

Royal Inn
30 Highway 70 W.
Hickory, NC 28602
(828) 322-4311
30 Rooms
TV/cable

Scottish Inn
325 Highway 70 W.
Hickory, NC 28602
(828) 328-2111
(828) 328-2111 (fax)
132 Rooms
Nonsmoking rooms, outdoor pool, handicapped accessible rooms, TV/cable, bar/lounge, pets allowed, complimentary coffee in lobby, newspaper, horseshoes,
some data ports, meeting rooms available

Sleep Inn
1179 13th Avenue Drive S.E.
Hickory, NC 28602
(828) 323-1140
(828) 324-6203 (fax)
www.hgmhotels.com
100 Rooms
Nonsmoking rooms, handicapped rooms, TV/cable, dry
cleaning/laundry service available weekdays, guest
laundry, complimentary deluxe continental breakfast,
complimentary *USA Today* newspaper Monday–Friday, free local calls, VCRs, data ports at work desk
with special lighting, pool and exercise room shared
with Comfort Suites, meeting rooms available

Super 8
312 N. Oxford Street
Claremont, NC 28610
(828) 459-7777
(828) 459-2037 (fax)
60 Rooms
Nonsmoking rooms, outdoor pool, health club, handicap
rooms, pets allowed, TV/cable, guest laundry, compli-

---

*"I'm sure you've heard this before but I'm telling you because it
happens time and again: Take your measurements! Measure
your front door, measure your staircase, measure the height of
the windows, because once you get it home, whether it's a custom sofa or a china cabinet (and 80 percent of orders are custom), it's yours and we can't take it back whether it fits up your
spiral staircase or not."* —DALE GREENWOOD, PRESIDENT, BLOW-
ING ROCK FURNITURE COMPANY

mentary continental breakfast, refrigerator, coffeepot, hairdryer, full-length mirror, data ports, free local calls, meeting rooms available

Trott House Inn Bed & Breakfast
802 N. Main Avenue
Newton, NC 28658
(828) 465-0404
(828) 465-5753 (fax)
www.trotthouse.com

DINING

Even more so than High Point, Hickory is dominated by chain and generic restaurants. There are a few nice places with local character, indicated by an ⇥, but for the most part you'll be choosing from a predictable roster of fare. Still, there's something to be said for predictability, and Hickory has the advantage of easy-to-find, modern, quick, clean restaurants aplenty. You won't starve in Hickory, not by a long shot.

Key
$ Dirt cheap
$$ Inexpensive to moderate
$$$ Moderate
$$$$ Expensive

American-Continental

⇥ **1859 Café**
443 2nd Avenue S.W., Hickory, (828) 322-1859
$$$
One of the better and more elegant restaurants in the
area, serving contemporary American cuisine

14th Avenue Cafe & Grill
288 14th Avenue N.E., Hickory, (828) 322-5336
$

Applebee's Neighborhood Grill & Bar
2180 Highway 70 S.E., Hickory, (828) 328-1000
$$

Arizona's Southwest Grill
1423 29th Avenue Drive N.E., Hickory, (828) 256-5644
$$$

Backstreets Bar & Grill
246 14th Avenue N.E., Hickory, (828) 328-6479
$$

Blues Room, The
10 2nd Street N.W., Hickory, (828) 322-4922
$$

Café 2 Forty 2
242 11th Avenue N.E., Hickory, (828) 324-2005
$$$

"The more prepared you are as a shopper, the better equipped we'll be to help you choose the furniture you'll be happy with in the long term. It all starts with narrowing down the field: What are your likes and dislikes? It's more efficient to know what you do like, but even if you only know what you don't like it's a place for us to start." —TIM SHEPARD, CAREER SALESMAN (MORE THAN 25 YEARS), ROSE FURNITURE COMPANY

Carolina Bagel Bakery
1131 2nd Street N.E., Hickory, (828) 328-6116
$

Charolais Steak House
766 4th Street Drive S.W., Hickory, (828) 328-4597
$$$

Cracker Barrel
1250 11th Street Court S.E., Hickory, (828) 261-0508
$$$

Flapjack's
3140 Oxford Street, Claremont, (828) 459-9288
$$

Fuddruckers
1510 8th Street Drive S.E., Hickory, (828) 323-1044
$$

Garden Café The,
403 Highway 70 S.W., Hickory, (828) 324-2232
$$

Golden Corral
1050 Lenoir-Rhyne Blvd. S.E., Hickory, (828) 324-2122
$$

Ham's
204 Highway 321 N.W., Hickory, (828) 326-4267
$

Hickory Tavern Grill & Raw Bar
2710 N. Center Street, Hickory, (828) 325-0991
$$$

IHOP
2415 Highway 70 S.E., Hickory, (828) 261-0150
$$

J & S Cafeteria, Inc.
13th Avenue Drive S.E., Hickory, (828) 326-8926
$$

Joel's Kitchen
2145 N. Center Street, Hickory, (828) 327-4816
$

Mario's & Jeni's
2289 St. Paul's Church Road, Newton, (828) 465-3177
$$$

McGuffey's Restaurant
1350 Highway 321 N.W., Hickory, (828) 327-6600
$$$

Mister Omelet
820 Highway 70 S.W. at Highway 321, Hickory
(828) 327-9537
$

Outback Steakhouse
1435 13th Avenue Drive S.E., Hickory, (828) 328-6283
$$$

Peddler Steak House
1180 Lenoir-Rhyne Blvd. S.E., Hickory, (828) 261-0401
$$$

Riverchase Restaurant
6610 Highway 16 N., Conover, (828) 256-1646
$$$

Rock-Ola Café
1185 Lenoir-Rhyne Blvd. S.E., Hickory, (828) 324-1828
$$$

Ruby Tuesday's
1825 Highway 70 S.E., Hickory, (828) 267-2981
$$

Sagebrush
1520 Highway 70 S.E., Hickory, (828) 327-2892
1420 2nd Street N.E., Hickory, (828) 322-1137
$$$

Schlotzsky's Deli
1322 Highway 70 S.E., Hickory, (828) 267-0905
$$

Snack Bar
1346 1st Avenue S.W., Hickory, (828) 322-5432
$$

Steak & Ale
1345 Lenoir-Rhyne Blvd. S.E., Hickory, (828) 322-8597
$$$

Stockyard & Company Grille
3441 N. Highway 16, Conover
(828) 465-9976
$$$

↠ **Vintage House, The**
271 3rd Avenue N.W., Hickory, (828) 324-1210
$$$$
A local institution for fine dining

Western Steer
321 and Highway 10 Intersection, Newton
(828) 464-8054
1190 Lenoir-Rhyne Blvd. S.E., Hickory, (828) 328-5062
$$

Asian

Dragon Palace
924 Conover Blvd., Conover, (828) 465-0964
$$

Ginza Japanese Restaurant
2065 Highway 70 S.E., Hickory, (828) 328-6882
$$$

Kobe Japanese
1103 13th Avenue S.E., Hickory, (828) 328-5688
$$$

Osaka Japanese Cuisine
3232 Springs Road N.E., Hickory, (828) 441-2495
$$

Barbecue

Bennett's Smokehouse & Saloon
1819 Fairgrove Church Road, Conover, (828) 464-6967
$$

Carolina Country BBQ
2060 Highway 70 S.E., Hickory, (828) 345-1246
$

Hannah's Bar-B-Que
709 9th Street S.W., Hickory, (828) 322-3711
2942 N. Oxford Street, Claremont, (828) 459-9889
$

Hickory Smokehouse
Highway 127 Viewmont, Hickory, (828) 328-2300
$

Brew Pub

Olde Hickory Tap Room
222 Union Square, Hickory, (828) 322-1965
$$

Italian/Pizza

Geppeto's Pizza
1030 N.E. 16th Street, Hickory, (828) 328-8818
$$

Giovanni's of Hickory
2601 N. Center Street, Hickory, (828) 322-8277
$$

Olive Garden
2261 Highway 70 S.E., Hickory, (828) 345-1015
$$$

Pizza Hut
2321 N. Center Street, Hickory, (828) 322-5984
$$

Ragazzi's
1770 Highway 70 S.E., Hickory, (828) 328-2558
$$$

Turn 4 Pizza
3200 Highway 127 S., Hickory, (828) 294-3663
$$

Village Inn Pizza Parlor
326 Highway 70 S.W., Hickory, (828) 328-3010
$$

Latin/Mexican/Southwestern

Dos Amigos
3133 Highway 70 S.E., Hickory, (828) 466-1920
$$

El Chapala
1205 2nd Street N.E., Hickory, (828) 324-7764
$$

El Sombrero Restaurant
909 8th Avenue N.E., Hickory, (828) 328-4220
$$

Max' Mexican Eatery
802 Highway 70 S.W., Hickory, (828) 322-6147
2220 N. Center Street, Hickory, (828) 328-5040
$$

Seafood

Captain's Galley
1261 16th Street N.E., Hickory, (828) 327-0555
$$$

Libby Hill Family Fish House
2255 Highway 70 S.E., Hickory, (828) 327-6696
$$

Mom's Seafood Kitchen
105 E. Main Street, Claremont, (828) 459-7732
$$

Red Lobster
1846 Highway 70 S.E., Hickory, (828) 327-6113
$$$

Quick Bites

Custard and Crème
2237 Highway 70 S.E., Hickory, (828) 328-7328
$

Emerson's Coffee & Tea Emporium
Valley Hills Mall, Hickory, (828) 328-1092
$

Krispy Kreme
1700 Highway 70 S.E., Hickory, (828) 326-9174
$

ATTRACTIONS

Acoustic Stage
(828) 324-5951

Twenty-five concerts and performances annually, by nationally known artists. At the Arts & Science Center Auditorium and the Hickory Community Theatre Firemen's Kitchen.

Bunker Hill Covered Bridge
14 miles east of Hickory off Highway 70, in Claremont
(828) 465-0383

One of only two covered bridges remaining in North
Carolina; built in 1895, the bridge's 85-foot span
crosses Lyles Creek
www.catawbahistory.org

Catawba County Museum of History
(828) 465-0383
Housed in the old 1924 Catawba County Courthouse,
the museum has an interesting collection of local artifacts ranging from a Revolutionary-era British red-
coat to a 1930's race car to, of course, furniture; closed
Mondays
www.catawbahistory.org/museum.htm

Catawba Science Center
243 Third Avenue N.E.
(828) 322-8169
The Center's participatory exhibits are designed to make
learning fun, and there's also a great gift shop; in the
Arts and Science Center of the Catawba Valley
Admission $2 for adults; $1 for youth under age 16 and
seniors; free for members and for children under age
three
Tuesday–Friday, 10:00 AM–5:00 PM; Saturday, 10:00
AM–4:00 PM; Sunday, 1:00 PM–4:00 PM; closed
Mondays
www.catawbascience.org

Catawba Valley Furniture Museum
Hickory Furniture Mart, 2220 Highway 70 E.
(828) 322-3510
If you're going to be in the Mart anyway, as you likely
will be, check out this exhibit, which includes a reproduction of an early woodworking shop complete with
vintage tools

Monday–Saturday, 9:00 AM–6:00 PM
www.hickoryfurniture.com

Firefighters Museum of Catawba County
3957 Herman Sipe Road, Conover
(828) 466-0911
Items on display include six fire trucks, including a 1936
    American LaFrance pumper
Free admission (donations accepted)
Open to the public Saturdays, 11:00 AM–4:00 PM;
    Sundays, 1:00 PM–4:00 PM

Fort Defiance
Highway 268, Lenoir (off Highway 321)
(828) 758-1671
The 18th-century home of General William Lenoir,
    beautifully restored
Open April through October

Green Room Community Theatre
60 W. Sixth Street, Newton
(828) 464-6128
A respected community theater group, with performances
    at the Newton-Conover Civic & Performance Place

"It's important to trust the salespeople who are working with you. Every salesperson in town knows that all it takes is one cocktail party to ruin his or her reputation. Here, furniture sales is a career, not just a stop on the way to another job. Your salesperson really wants to help you—has to help you—get what you need." —TODD KESTER, MANAGER AND FOURTH-GENERATION ROSE FURNITURE FAMILY

Hickory Community Theatre
In historic Old Hickory City Hall, 30 3rd Street N.W.,
   Hickory
(828) 327-3855
One of the better community theater groups in the area
www.hct.org

Hickory Crawdads Baseball
2500 Clement Blvd. N.W., off Highway 321; from I-40
   take exit 123 North, Hickory
(800) 488-DADS/(828) 322-3000
Class A minor-league team
www.hickorycrawdads.com

Hickory Motor Speedway
Highway 70 E., Newton
(828) 464-3655
The birthplace of, among others, NASCAR megastars
   Dale Earnhardt, Junior Johnson, Ned and Dale Jar-
   rett, and Harry Gant
Season runs March through October
www.hickoryspeedway.com

Hickory Museum of Art
243 Third Avenue N.E., Hickory
(828) 327-8576
Excellent collection of American art; located in the Arts
   and Science Center of Catawba Valley
Tuesday–Friday, 10:00 AM–5:00 PM; Saturday, 10:00
   AM–4:00 PM; Sunday, 1:00 PM–4:00 PM, closed
   Mondays
www.hickorymuseumofart.org

Ivey Arboretum in Carolina Park, The
Adjacent to downtown Hickory on N.C. Highway 127
   North

(828) 323-7500/(828) 322-7046

A collection of over 400 species of native and rare trees and shrubs, all clearly labeled, in a three-acre park; recently restored

www.ci.hickory.nc.us/publicsvcs/iveyarboretum.htm

Lenoir-Rhyne College Summer Theatre, The

(828) 328-7230

Performances in late July and early August in the Belk Centrum on the Lenoir-Rhyne Campus

Terrell Country Store

Corner of Highway 150 and Sherrills Ford Road

(828) 478-2065

An 1891 country store, which was a major center of trade in the area and also the post office for more than a century

www.catawbahistory.org

Waldensian Heritage Wines

4940 Villar Lane N.E., Valdese

(828) 879-3202

North Carolina is home to a number of wineries, and this one is open for tours and tastings every Friday, Saturday, and Sunday from 1:00 PM until 6:00 PM

Waldensian Museum

208 Rodoret Street S.E., Valdese

(828) 874-2531

The Waldenses are a sect with roots in the Protestant Reformation

www.waldensianpresbyterian.com/museum.htm

Western Piedmont Symphony

243 3rd Avenue N.E., Hickory

(828) 324-8603

A delightful symphony with some strong guest
    performers
www.wpsymphony.org

FAMILY AMUSEMENT

Hickory Dickory Dock
825 Highway 70 S.E., Hickory
(828) 322-3625
Family entertainment center with 33,000 square feet of
    indoor activities, including bumper cars, minigolf, soft
    modular play, two laser arenas, restaurant, birthday
    party rooms, covered picnic areas, over 100 arcade
    games, and a redemption prize center
Monday Thursday, 10:00 AM–10:00 PM; Friday–Satur-
    day, 10:00 AM–11:00 PM; Sunday, 12:00 PM–8:00 PM
www.hickory-dickory-dock.com

Ice Castle Skating Rink
1901-N N.W. Blvd., Newton
(828) 466-1173
Public skating, free-style sessions, and lessons with
    American Open Professional Pair Champions Kim
    and Gray Johnson
Tuesday–Thursday, 3:00 PM–8:30 PM; Friday, 3:00
    PM–11:00 PM; Saturday, 11:00 AM–11:00 PM; Sunday,
    1:30 PM–6:00 PM

Pin Station
525 W. A Street, Newton
(828) 466-2695
42 lanes, game room, pool tables, and snack bar
Monday–Thursday, 8:00 AM–9:30 PM; Friday–Saturday,
    8:00 AM–1:30 AM; Sunday, 1:00 PM–10:00 PM

Rack n' Roll Billiards & Amusements
2180 Northwest Blvd., Newton
(828) 464-POOL
Alcohol-free
Monday–Thursday, 10:00 AM–9:00 PM; Friday–Saturday,
10:00 AM–11:00 PM; Sunday, 1:00 PM–8:00 PM

Skateland USA
2820 Highway 70 S.E., Newton
(828) 322-8824
Roller skating, video games, and parties
Open Monday–Saturday

ATTRACTIONS FARTHER AFIELD

If you're going to be in Western North Carolina, it would be a shame not to visit some of the amazing attractions in that part of the state. These are the best of the best, each of which is well worth a day trip. In addition, consider just visiting the lovely, artsy, hip town of Asheville (and especially its world famous farmer's market), due west of Hickory on I-40.

➻ **Biltmore Estate**
   Open daily 9:00 AM–5:00 PM, closed Thanksgiving and
      Christmas Day
   Tickets and information: (800) 624-1304
   www.biltmore.com

The largest private residence in the nation, Biltmore Estate is a French Renaissance-style château built by the grandson of tycoon George Vanderbilt in 1895. It is chock-full of art and antiques, and surrounded by gorgeous formal gardens. Biltmore Estate is a national historic landmark and must be seen to be believed. There is also a winery with a visitor's center, tasting room, and retail store. It took 1,000 men six years to build the château. It has more than four acres of floor space, 250 rooms, 65 fireplaces, 43 bathrooms, 34 bedrooms, and three kitchens. The Banquet Hall's table could seat 64 guests, who were served eight-course meals requiring 15 utensils per person to eat.

⤛ Great Smoky Mountains National Park
107 Park Headquarters
Gatlinburg, TN 37738
(615) 436-1200
www.nps.gov/grsm/gsmsite/home/

Established in 1934, this is America's most popular national park, and half of its 520,408 acres are in North Carolina (the rest is in neighboring Tennessee). It's an ideal place to camp, fish, hike, horseback ride, and relax. The Oconaluftee Visitor Center, near Cherokee, N.C., is open year-round. It offers exhibits focusing on mountain life of the late 1800s. Next to the visitor center is the Mountain Farm Museum. From I-40, take U.S. Route 19 West through Maggie Valley, to U.S. 441 North at Cherokee and into the Park.

⤛ North Carolina Zoological Park
4401 Zoo Parkway
Asheboro, NC 27203
Information: (336) 879-7000
www.nczoo.org

Located in Asheboro, the North Carolina Zoological Park is the world's largest natural habitat zoo. Among many other things, it features an African region with eight outdoor exhibits and more than 200 animals; the R.J. Reynolds Aviary with free-flying birds; and the wonderful warthog exhibit.

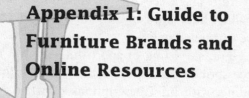

Appendix 1: Guide to Furniture Brands and Online Resources

The World Wide Web is such an amazing tool for the furniture shopper, it's hard to imagine how people shopped for furniture before the advent of the computer. Without leaving your desk, you can see photographs of just about every piece of furniture you could conceivably buy in North Carolina. This makes planning and strategizing so much easier, I'd almost recommend buying a computer with Internet access just for this purpose if you don't already own one (and hey, if you're really planning to buy a lot of furniture, the money you save by shopping in North Carolina will actually pay for the cost of your new computer).

Throughout this book, any retailer, outlet, or clearance center that has a Web site is included in its listing. Some of those sites contain extensive online catalogs, but of course the catalogs are limited to the lines any given store carries. Many furniture and accessories manufacturers, however, make their product lines and company information available directly to the consumer, online.

Here is a listing of approximately 100 key furniture and accessories manufacturers that make information available online, with brief descriptions of what each manufacturer offers. If you see something you like, the next step is to find a store in North Carolina that carries and displays it. Many manufacturers list their authorized dealers right on their Web sites, or you can e-mail for the information. In addition, the major lines carried by each store are included in the Hickory and High Point listings sections of this book. And don't forget, many manufacturers make furniture in similar styles. So if you see something you like, you may be able to find a similar piece made by a different manufacturer—and you may even save a little money on account of your flexibility and imagination.

ACTION INDUSTRIES

www.action-lane.com
Part of the Lane empire, Action Industries includes all varieties of reclining furniture, most notably the traditional "man in front of the ballgame" recliners. But these recliners are anything but ordinary: Great leaps in technology have been made so that it's not just dad sitting in the recliners anymore, but anyone and everyone interested in kicking back and putting their feet up. Lane has recliners and gliders, recliners for small people and for big people. How does the "Rhino" or the "Grandeur" sound? These are chairs specifically designed for comfort and durability. Maybe it's a massage recliner or a

Tempur-Rest™ you prefer. If it involves action furniture, this is certainly a good place to start.

AMERICAN DREW

www.americandrew.com
It's all about value with American Drew. Known for the Cherry Grove collection (traditional) since 1960, there's plenty more to choose from, whether it's country oak or contemporary wood styles. Dining room and bedroom sets are available in most collections and some even include entertainment centers and wall units. A solid, mid-priced manufacturer.

ANDREW PEARSON

www.andrewpearsondesign.com
Contemporary furniture that could pinch-hit as art, Andrew Pearson Design is all about the glass design and the whimsy of the customer. Each piece can be adapted to fit your specifications or space restrictions. So, in essence, your piece is your very own—an original.

ARTISTICA METAL DESIGNS

www.artisticametal.com
An extensive, quality collection of iron occasional furniture from beds and baker's racks to occasional tables and casual dining sets.

ASHLEY FURNITURE INDUSTRIES

www.ashleyfurniture.com
Every room in the house is covered with the selection from Ashley, from kids' rooms to wall units, dining rooms to dens.

The furniture is value priced and is great for families on a budget.

BAKER

www.bakerfurniture.com
Baker has been manufacturing furniture since 1893 in collections of living room, dining room, bedroom, occasional, and upholstered furniture. Everything from home furnishings—beds, tables, chairs, sofas, armoires, and cabinets—to the more recent additions of executive office furnishings. It's "furniture to grow more beautiful in use, in this generation and the next."

BARCALOUNGER FURNITURE COMPANY

www.barcalounger.com
Upholstery manufacturer specializing in motion recliners, gliders, high-leg loungers, sofas, love seats, and sectionals. Choose from traditional, contemporary, and wicker styles, many with optional finishes and nail-head trim. Another comfort favorite.

BENCHCRAFT

www.benchcraft.com
"Welcome home to a world of comfort." The slogan says it all: Benchcraft specializes in upholstered, casual, and comfort-oriented furniture. Recliners, sleepers, and sectionals in fabric and leather—all in casually stylish selections.

BENTWOOD FURNITURE, INC.

www.bentwoodfurn.com
Since 1970 the entrepreneurs at Bentwood set a standard by

utilizing gas, rather than the traditional steam method, to bend wood to realize their vision in case goods furnishings. Dining rooms, hutches, bookcases, bar stools, chairs, oak accessories, roll-top desks, and entertainment centers in American country and traditional styles are amongst this manufacturer's selections.

BERKLINE

www.berkline.com

With over 50 years of experience designing and manufacturing motion furniture, it's not hard to see why Berkline continues to be a pioneer in the field. Whether it's the Shiatsu massage recliner in a variety of different styles and fabrics, the EasyLift™ to help you into or out of your recliner, or a straightforward comfort recliner, Berkline has all the bases covered for selection and quality. Berkline also has sofas and sectionals for every need from Home Theater to contemporary and country—in leather, too.

BERMEX

www.bermex.ca

Founded in 1983, Bermex has expanded to manufacture case goods in casual and formal furnishings from occasional pieces like kitchen islands, dining rooms, bedrooms, and bar stools. You choose from 52 finishes to personalize your selection whether you opt for contemporary, Mission, Shaker, Louis Philippe, Deco, or country.

BERNHARDT

www.bernhardt.com

Founded in 1889, the Bernhardt Furniture Company is one of the largest family owned and operated manufacturers of fine case goods and upholstered furniture in the United States. Located in the foothills of Western North Carolina, Bernhardt employs over 2,000 people and this manufacturer has something for everyone, whether you prefer classic designs, contemporary styles, or something in between. It's furniture that's built to last and meant to add character and grow with you in your home.

BEST CHAIRS

www.bestchairs.com
Since 1962 the guys (founded by three guys) at Best have been working to bring customers a combination of comfort and value. They've evolved and expanded quite a bit since that time but still hold fast to that original objective. Selections include glide rockers (wood), swivel gliders, wing chairs, club chairs, recliners, sofas, chairs, and office furniture.

BRADINGTON YOUNG

www.bradington-young.com
Quality speaks for itself—hardwood frames, double-doweled glued and screwed corner blocks, double-cone coil spring construction—and Bradington Young fills the bill. Sectionals and lounge chairs, recliners, love seats, and sleepers, motion and stationary sofas; this is upholstered motion and comfort furniture of upper-end quality and styling. Some recliners feature intricate ball-and-claw carved feet and brass nail trim, others offer the option of wall-hugging, swivel, glider, recliner, and pop-up headrests. Leather (more than 100 selections), upholstery (over 250 to choose from), and leather-vinyl combos are available in recline and incline options, all with limited lifetime warranties on the reclining mechanism, wood frame parts, and seat cushion cores.

BRASSCRAFTERS

www.bardintl.com/brass.htm
It's all about accessorizing at Brasscrafters, from antique silver, brass, and pewter to picture frames, candleholders, boxes, bookends, statues, and sconces.

BRAXTON CULLER

www.braxtonculler.com
Quality wicker/rattan and upholstered furniture, Braxton Culler (since 1975) is a High Point original manufacturer. Selections include armoires, dining room and bedroom collections, étagères, sleepers, love seats, recliners, and occasional tables. Every line can be tailored to your personal specifications to blend fabrics, leather, wood, and wicker with a variety of colors and finishes.

BROYHILL

www.broyhillfurn.com
One of the largest furniture manufacturers in the world and a well-recognized name in furniture, Broyhill has something for every taste whether it's traditional or contemporary bedroom, living room, home office, home theater, or dining room. Prices fall in the middle range from medium-low to middle-medium. Broyhill is a favorite brand amongst shoppers in this price category and held to a standard defining its reputation, it offers quality, fashion, and style to its customers.

C.R. LAINE

www.crlaine.com
C.R. Laine, a family owned and operated company since 1958, offers a selection of quality upholstered furniture com-

prising, as is stated in Laine's mission, "fashion, comfort, service and affordability." If it involves seating, you should be able to get it from Laine, whether it's a sleeper, a rocker, a sofa, sectional or love seat. There are hundreds of choices for frames and fabrics, enabling the customer to create each piece to personal specifications.

CAMBRIDGE LAMPS

www.cambridgelamps.com
Since 1935 Cambridge Lamps has been designing and crafting lighting products by hand. Whether your taste runs to contemporary or traditional, lighting, like the furniture industry, is always changing and evolving and Cambridge covers all the bases to meet varying needs. You've got to figure, if it's good enough for the White House, it's probably good enough for you. Cambridge is used in homes, hotels, resorts, and businesses around the globe. Also a manufacturer of home accessories, mirrors, and occasional tables.

CAPEL RUGS

www.capelrugs.com
Started in 1917 by A. Leon Capel to supply braided rugs, Capel is now the largest and oldest supplier of area rugs in America. But Capel knows that, "big and old don't make you good." To stay on top of the competition and keep its coveted number one slot, a family member runs every area of the Capel operation from manufacturing to importing. The company's philosophy has remained the same for over 80 years: "Styles and tastes change; appreciation for quality does not." Choices include more than 100 different rug styles and hundreds of colors. Each style is offered in a large range of sizes and you can also special-order a custom size.

CARSON'S

www.carsonsofhp.com
Since 1944 Carson's has been catering to the trends and needs of the customer. A medium-priced contemporary upholstery and occasional furniture manufacturer, Carson's focuses on style and delivers comfort.

CENTURY FURNITURE COMPANY

www.centuryfurniture.com
A company with such pride in its products that every employee has a stake in the business, this quality manufacturer offers case goods and upholstered furniture in styles ranging from contemporary to reproduction. The choices are incredible: the upholstery division offers dozens of finishes and many hundreds of fabrics to choose from; the case goods division specializes in bedroom, dining room, and occasional furnishings with well over ten collections and dozens of finishes to choose from; and not to be overlooked, the leather division offers recliners and sectionals in a variety of quality leathers.

CHAPMAN

www.chapmanco.com
It's about lighting and accessorizing at Chapman. With over 1,000 designs to choose from in chandeliers, table and floor lamps, sconces, decorative accessories, and accent furniture, you'll find yourself in good company with other Chapman customers including the White House, royal palaces, embassies, ocean liners, and executive offices.

CHARLESTON FORGE

www.charlestonforge.com
Handsome and innovative handcrafted iron and wood furniture.

CLASSIC GALLERY

www.classicgallery.com
It's difficult not to recognize quality when you see it, especially with upholstered seating where the mechanisms are invisible. But with the four Classic Gallery companies—Classic Gallery, Classic Traditions, Ecco Design, and Classic Gallery Contract—all of your bases are covered, whether it's contemporary or traditional upholstery that you want. One especially unique and outstanding feature Classic offers is the option to design the actual size of your seating—including sectionals, sofas, chairs, ottomans, and chaises—to your unique specifications. You want that sofa to be a sleeper with a small skirt? It's your furniture, and it's your choice. As they say at Classic: "Don't you look for shoes that fit? Why not furniture?" What more can you ask for?

CLASSIC LEATHER

www.classic-leather.com
If it exists in leather seating, you'll be hard-pressed not to find it from Classic Leather: Wing chairs, bar stools, occasional chairs, lounge chairs, office and executive seating, all available in more than 20 leather selections and over 170 colors. This family and employee-owned furniture manufacturer has been around since 1966.

CLAYTON MARCUS

www.claytonmarcus.com
There is a range in quality at Clayton Marcus (a medium- to medium-upper-priced manufacturer) but all of the furnishings feature the trappings of quality production: eight-way double-cone springs in the seats, 5/4 double-doweled, glued and screwed joints, and generous padding and cushioning on

corners, arms, and backs. Whether it's a casual recliner or a leather sofa, your seating is held to a high standard of quality.

COCHRANE FURNITURE

www.cochrane-furniture.com
Established in 1900 to successfully produce "trainloads" of fireplace mantels, Cochrane now manufactures bedroom, living room, and dining room furnishings from maple, oak, cherry, and ash. Solid tops, sides, and fronts and solid wood drawer glides with floating case construction speak quality and pride.

COLONIAL FURNITURE COMPANY

www.colonialfurniture.com
Bedroom, dining room, and occasional furniture in Appalachian wild cherry and red oak are the specialty of the house from this family owned manufacturer. Whether it's formal and traditional 18th-century designs or informal and casual country styles, each product is carefully constructed of solid wood.

COUNCILL CRAFTSMEN, INC.

www.councill.com
Established in 1973 by Fred and Hope Councill, this high-end quality manufacturer started out with 18th-century reproductions and has since expanded to include upholstery, seating, executive furniture, and other styles in case goods.

COX MANUFACTURING

www.coxmfg.com
Established in 1932, Cox has been consistent in its successful line of fully upholstered accent furniture. Product categories

include: chaise lounges, love seats, chairs and ottomans, boudoir chairs, wing chairs, host and hostess chairs, side chairs, bar stools, cocktail ottomans, benches, revolving stools, storage accents and hassocks, pillows, table skirts and screens, and a wide variety of wrought-iron furniture.

CRAFTIQUE

www.craftiquefurn.com

An artisanal manufacturer of traditional English and American styles of solid mahogany bedroom, dining room, and accent furniture since 1946, Craftique takes pride in being behind the times in manufacturing technology so the art is still in every aspect of the production—right down to the final finish. Back panels are fastened with brass screws instead of staples, every drawer bottom is "blocked," all sides of cabinets are hand rubbed (not just the top), drawer fronts are fully rabbetted, and joints are English dovetail. The finishes are meant to last many lifetimes, so Craftique furniture can be handed down from one generation to the next.

DAWSON FURNITURE COMPANY

www.dawsonfurniture.com

The distinguishing factor at Dawson would have to be the selection of curio cabinets constructed of glass and wood—of which there are almost 20 to choose from in a variety of finishes, woods, and sizes. Dawson also produces armoires, entertainment centers, home office and computer centers, steamer trunks, and RealWood ready-to-assemble furniture.

DREXEL HERITAGE

www.drexelheritage.com

Drexel (established in 1903) and Heritage (established in 1932 and acquired by Drexel in 1956) are together one of the world's top furniture manufacturers (when comparing size and volume). The longstanding reputation of Drexel Heritage as a manufacturer of fine furniture and quality craftsmanship continues to keep the company out front as an industry leader within middle- and upper-end manufacturing segments. Drexel Heritage includes residential product brands Drexel Heritage and Lillian August, and a contract business, Drexel Heritage Furnishings, Inc.

ELLIOTT'S DESIGNS

www.elliottsdesign.com
Handcrafted brass beds in a selection of styles and finishes are what distinguish the line from Elliott's. Also look for daybeds and accessories.

ELLO

www.ellofurniture.com
Established in 1954, Ello was a contemporary furniture pioneer in the United States and continues to stay out front. The selections include contemporary bedrooms, dining rooms, wall units, entertainment centers, and vitrines (curio cabinet in my book) in a variety of materials from wood and wood veneers, to glass and metal. Ello also distributes the Pietro Costantini line of contemporary chairs from Italy, the Marble-Italia line of marble dining and occasional tables from Italy, and Ello's Dining Room Collection, made exclusively in Italy for Ello.

EMERSON ET CIE

www.emersonetcie.com
Quality accessory and occasional line, Emerson Et Cie touts

"accents today, heirlooms tomorrow" and the products live up to the claim—if you care to share them.

FAIRFIELD CHAIR

www.fairfieldchair.com
Established in 1921, the Fairfield Chair Company is a family business that continues to be run and operated by what is now third-generation family. Fairfield offers more than 400 frames and over 5,000 different fabrics and leathers—plus the option for COM if you want to customize in the extreme. Quality is high for the price point: frames are made of kiln-dried hardwoods with triple-doweled joints, the swivel rocker's base features 49 ball bearings, five springs, and 2,000-pound breaking strength on the tabs. Not too shabby.

FAITH WALK DESIGNS

www.faithwalkdesigns.com
Faith Walk Designs, a subsidiary of Decorize, Inc., along with Decorize.com and GuildMaster *(www.guildmasterinc.com)*, specializes in hand-painted and heirloom-finished furniture and accessories. Each collection is designed by artist Mike Sandel and carefully recreated by artisans one piece at a time.

FICKS REED COMPANY

www.ficksreed.com
Wicker and rattan furnishings with custom finishes are what distinguish this 100-plus-year-old company from the rest. Dining room (more than 50 styles of dining chairs), bedroom, seating (love seats, sofas, and chairs), tables, and chests—just looking at the selections conjures up images of tropical paradise.

FLEXSTEEL

www.flexsteel.com

The Flexsteel company has a long (since 1893) and successful history, but it wasn't until 1913–1919 that the company started using steel frames, and 1958 that the company was so named. Flexsteel specializes in fine seating with the distinctive characteristic of its unique steel frames. An innovator in seating both for home use and transportation, Flexsteel is also responsible for seating in recreational vehicles like the famed Winnebago brand, has received endorsements from the International Chiropractors Association for its Ergo Touch adjustable lumbar support system, and the list goes on. If it's seating and it's comfortable and innovative, it's a good bet that you're sitting on Flexsteel.

FREDERICK COOPER

www.frederickcooper.com

Established in 1923 by Frederick Cooper, a Chicago artist, the company is known for its artistic originality and quality in lamps and lighting. Pieces are made one at time and signature treatments include the use of distinguished and exotic materials (like silk) to produce the company's renowned hand-sewn lampshades.

FREMARC DESIGNS

www.fremarc.com

Quality traditional and transitional furnishings in artful collections including Chateau, Country French, Renaissance, Country English, and Carved French. Lines include seating, bedroom, dining room, and occasional furnishing selections; options in size, finishes (standard, premium, or custom), and tabletop preferences (plain wood, burl, parquet, tudor, and beveled glass) are all a part of creating furniture that is uniquely yours.

GEORGE KOVACS

www.georgekovacs.com
Contemporary lighting so tasteful, it doesn't offend the senses of the traditionalist (is it even conceivable?). These lamps, lights, and fixtures stand on their own like art—because that's what they are.

GUY CHADDOCK & COMPANY

www.guychaddock.com
Antique reproductions come naturally to Guy Chaddock, who started restoring antiques and crafting one-of-a-kind reproductions more than 40 years ago. Today, master craftsmen continue to construct and finish each item to order—including armoires, entertainment centers, servers, sideboards, secretary desks, dining tables, dressers, consoles, cocktail tables, and computer cabinets (to name a few)—creating quality home furnishings that will last long enough to share.

HABERSHAM

www.habershamplantation.com
Started by a single mother who had fallen upon hard times, Habersham has come a long way since its modest beginnings of cigar box purses in 1972. Now Habersham offers hundreds of designs to choose from—the line has grown to encompass more than 400 individual pieces. Each piece is meticulously painted and handcrafted by the team of 135 (and growing) craftspeople and artisans who work together to create the Habersham line.

HALE

www.halebookcases.com
Since 1907 Hale has been a quality manufacturer of bookcases with tremendous pride in the creation and outcome of the finished product. There is a wide selection of finishes to choose from for the bookcases, which are available in oak, basswood, cherry, butternut, birch, and walnut. To support the local economy, virtually all lumber is purchased from loggers within a 75-mile radius of the manufacturer's original location in Herkimer, N.Y., and all wood is dried to precision in kilns maintained by Hale.

HAMMARY FURNITURE COMPANY

www.hammary.com
A division of La-Z-Boy, offering a variety of styles in occasional tables, home office, and upholstered furniture. Design styles run from traditional to contemporary.

HANCOCK & MOORE

www.hancockandmoore.com
High-quality seating—particularly leather—with an emphasis on the workmanship of skilled craftsmen and proven methods of construction that have withstood the test of time. For leather seating, you'll be hard-pressed to find a better price-to-quality ratio, and that's saying something.

HARDEN

www.harden.com
Harden, which includes Harden Residential and Harden Contract, is a fifth-generation family owned and operated

business. More than half of the 600 employees are actually related! And though that is both unique and special, that's only part of what sets Harden furniture apart. Harden offers furnishings for home (dining room, bedroom, occasional, home office, and upholstery) and office (case goods, seating, reception, conference, and hospitality) that are designed to fit your style and needs.

HEKMAN FURNITURE COMPANY

www.hekman.com

Since 1922 Hekman, originally a baker by trade, has been designing and manufacturing quality furniture that has evolved to include desks, occasional tables, wall units, entertainment centers, office furniture, and chairs in traditional and transitional styles. Exterior features include custom brass hardware, hand-fitted solid hardwood moldings, premium veneers, and solid hardwood panels. Product details that whisper quality include seven-ply drawer fronts, solid hardwood back and sides with dovetail construction, hardwood tongue and groove construction, solid hardwood legs doweled to rails and sides, and a five-ply top that prevents warping.

HENKEL HARRIS

www.henkelharris.com

Fine furniture since 1946, formal dining rooms (including china cabinets, sideboards, silver chests, chairs, and tables), exquisite bedrooms (beds, chests, armoires, entertainment centers, benches, dressers, and mirrors) and intricate occasional pieces (display cases, bar units, secretaries, end tables, consoles, bookcases, and cocktail tables) are all still meticulously manufactured in Virginia's Shenandoah Valley.

HENREDON

www.henredon.com

One of the best names in the business, with numerous lines and styles (European Formal, Timeless Classical, European Casual, Classic Traditional, Stylized Living, and Turn of the Century) to choose from—all of which are beautifully crafted and of excellent quality.

HICKORY CHAIR

www.hickorychair.com

Since 1911 Hickory Chair has stood for quality. With attention to details like shaped and kiln-dried hardwood frames, custom-engineered seating, four-way fabric matching, fully lined skirts, and fully wrapped frames, it's not hard to see why Hickory Chair remains a favorite. Extensive collections in leather and upholstery include the French Collection, the Mark Hampton Collection, the Mount Vernon Collection, Collector's Mix, the San Marino Collection, Grand Vista, and Winterthur Country Estate Collection.

HOMECREST

www.homecrest.com

Homecrest offers over 18 collections in aluminum and steel outdoor furniture including cushion, strap, and sling designs.

HOOKER FURNITURE

www.hookerfurniture.com

What is arguably the best quality-to-price ratio in the medium price range, Hooker has come to be known in the industry as a great value for the product. It's amazing that Hooker—from the employee stock ownership plan to the attention to detail and finishing—is able to produce the products that it does for the price you pay. More than one North Carolina career sales-person confided to me that in their opinion, you couldn't find a better furniture value for the price.

HOWARD MILLER

www.howardmiller.com
Earning the designation of "world's largest grandfather clock manufacturer" decades ago, Howard Miller also manufactur-ers tabletop, mantel, and wall clocks, as well as curio and dis-play cases for collectibles.

JASPER CABINET

www.jaspercabinetcompany.com
Established in 1904, Jasper is a world leader in secretaries, quality curio cabinets, desks, entertainment furniture, gun cabinets, and accent chests.

KINCAID

www.kincaidfurniture.com
A La-Z-Boy company (a name that speaks for itself), Kincaid produces quality furniture in over 20 collections including the Laura Ashley collection, Kings Road, Belle Maison, Common-wealth Cherry, and Hunter's Run.

KINGSDOWN MATTRESS COMPANY

www.kingsdown.com
Kingsdown has created sleep systems designed to provide the healthiest sleep possible—a far cry from the materials used when the company was established in 1904 (think corn shucks

and horsehair insulation). More than 95 years later the state-of-the-art materials have evolved into space age technology but Kingsdown mattress sets are still crafted by hand—often by descendants of Kingsdown's first employees.

KUSHWOOD MFG.

www.kushwood.com
Kushwood offers bar stools, bedrooms, dining rooms, bookcases, entertainment centers, office furniture, curio cabinets, and occasional tables to customers with discerning budgets.

LA BARGE

www.labargeinc.com
La Barge, a highly regarded upper-end manufacturer, specializes in Continental European-style furnishings including chairs, occasional tables, accessories, and mirrors.

LANE ACTION

www.actionlane.com
Motion furniture in every possible permutation—recliners, incliners, sleepers, sectionals—with hundreds of fabrics to choose from.

LANE FURNITURE INDUSTRIES

www.lanefurniture.com
Cedar chests are what the Lane Company originally became known for but there's a lot more to the company than chests for keepsakes and blankets. Established in 1912, Lane Furniture is now part of the impressive Furniture Brands International, which also owns Thomasville, Broyhill, and Lane Venture (see page 256). State-of-the-art technology and

recliners, Lane Leather, sleeper sofas, and sectionals are just a small part of what this company has come to represent.

LANE VENTURE

www.laneventure.com
Excursions, Weathermaster, Tradewinds, and Weathercraft are the lines that make up Lane Venture and include wicker selections for living and dining rooms with a variety of finishes and fabrics. Fully upholstered pieces offer options on skirts, fringe, and braids; and a unique design of vinyl wicker on aluminum frames for outdoors is weatherproof and cost efficient.

LEA INDUSTRIES

www.leaindustries.com
A La-Z-Boy company, Lea Industries is a leading manufacturer of reasonably priced youth furniture.

LEATHERCRAFT

www.leathercraft-furniture.com
Leathercraft uses only the finest quality materials—leathers from around the world and superior materials for seating including handmade frames and waterfowl down—to create a finished product that sets it apart from the pack.

LEXINGTON

www.lexington.com
One of the most popular and recognized names in middle- to high-end furniture, Lexington covers just about every imaginable home furnishing and home office need. Lexington produces furniture in a wide range of styles, including American and European traditional, 18th century, transitional, country, and

casual. Also known as the Lexington Home Brands Company, Lexington also has 12 branded (licensed) collections including Bob Timberlake® (the industry's best-selling collection of all time), Henry Link Trading Company™, Nautica Home, Palmer Home™, Smithsonian®, Southern Living®, Tommy Bahama®, Waverly®, and Lexington® (the umbrella brand for all other Lexington groups and categories); also, youth brands Betsy Cameron™, Lauryn Olivia™, and Lexington Kids™.

MAITLAND-SMITH

www.maitland–smith.com
Maitland-Smith is a premium manufacturer (and designer) of 17th–18th-century English-style furniture. Dining room tables, china cabinets, desks, game tables, and even entertainment centers (to name a few) are constructed with elaborate wood veneers. Mirrors, hanging art, curio cabinets, lighting, and chandeliers are also part of the selection.

MEADOWCRAFT

www.meadowcraft.com
Meadowcraft is the largest manufacturer of wrought-iron outdoor furniture in the country and is one of the country's leading manufacturers of casual outdoor furniture. Meadowcraft also designs, manufactures, and distributes outdoor and indoor wrought-iron products and accessories, outdoor cushions, and umbrellas.

MIKHAIL DARAFEEV

www.darafeev.com
Game tables, bar stools, bars, pub tables, and gaming sets, Darafeev makes all the components needed for a home recreation center.

MILLER DESK

www.millerdesk.com

A design pioneer (with the creation of the TV cabinet) and a manufacturing pioneer (an originator of "knock-down" furniture), Miller now has multiple divisions: Miller Desk makes computer work stations, conference and occasional tables, executive office furniture, bookcases, storage cabinets, and a tremendous selection of desks, chairs, and file cabinets. Miller Office Seating division makes over 500 basic styles of chairs offered in thousands of permutations of wood, finish, and fabric colors. And yes, combined there is knock-down television cabinetry.

MINOFF LAMP (KICHLER)

www.kichler.com

Established in 1938, Kichler remains a privately held, family owned and operated business that today is the largest decorative lighting fixture company in the world. Built on original, design-oriented, high-quality lighting products at competitive prices, Minoff's reputation is backed by educated and caring staff and an equally strong customer service team. Kichler® Lighting also happens to be a four-time winner of the Arts Award as Lighting Manufacturer of the Year, apparently the highest accolade the lighting industry can impart.

MOOSEHEAD FURNITURE COMPANY

www.mooseheadfurniture.com

Founded in Maine in 1947 by a pair of brothers, Moosehead Mfg. has grown by leaps and bounds since its humble beginnings and now encompasses bedroom, dining room, occasional, bookcases, desks, and rockers. Everything is constructed from northern hardwoods (like maple), though in the hopes of drawing in and keeping fresh customers Moosehead recently expanded its line to include infant, youth, and young adult furniture and its wood selection to include ash.

PALECEK

www.palecek.com
Established in 1975, Palecek delivers woven rattan to the American public and features wicker and woven designs in furniture, a line of accessories, as well as lighting.

PENNSYLVANIA HOUSE

www.pennsylvaniahouse.com
Pennsylvania House has been making furniture since 1892—far too long to be in business if the product weren't satisfying generations of customers. Selections include middle- to high-end case goods and upholstery pieces, American and traditional styles of bedroom, living room, and dining room furnishings in mahogany, oak, cherry, maple, and pine.

POWELL (LIFE CHEST)

www.lifechest.com
Powell has designed The Life Chest by Powell, an heirloom-quality chest designed with features to allow you to safely store life's precious mementos.

PULASKI

www.pulaskifurniture.com
Curios and collector's cabinets, corner cabinets, consoles, entertainment centers, armoires, bookcases, home office, and dining and bedroom sets are the furnishings that Pulaski offers in all shapes and sizes and in a multitude of finishes.

REPLOGLE GLOBES

www.replogleglobes.com
Since 1930 Replogle has introduced geographical globes into millions of homes, offices, and schools throughout the world. And, as the world evolves so does Replogle, keeping up with the times and trends and designing globes that are centerpieces, accessories, and heirlooms.

RICHARDSON BROS.

www.richardsonbrothers.com
Reputable and reliable dining furniture for over 150 years (since 1848), Richardson Bros. has a long tradition of making quality solid oak and cherry bedroom and dining room furniture. Lines include the Country Oak collection, Brownstone, the Missioncraft collection, the Door Country collection, and Home Basics.

RIVERSIDE FURNITURE

www.riverside-furniture.com
"We want the Riverside name to be trusted for quality products that are an affordable value. It's just that simple." And that's what the company founder, Herman Udouj, set as a goal and worked toward all those decades ago (1946)—and the modern company continues to strive toward and achieve that goal. Furniture selections include bedroom sets, home office, computer desks, credenzas, entertainment centers, rolltop desks, bookcases, occasional tables, desk chairs, casual dining, curio cabinets, and new seasonal selections.

ROBERT BERGELIN COMPANY

www.rbcfurn.com
One of the great small furniture manufacturers remaining in

North Carolina, Robert Bergelin is truly artisanal in every regard and only sells factory direct. With all the middlemen out of the picture, Bergelin's pieces wind up being relatively economical when compared to far inferior merchandise that costs nearly as much. All orders are custom, from design preferences to the finish on the wood. True heirloom furniture, the tables are particularly beautiful, and custom requests of all kinds are happily accommodated.

ROXTON TEMPLE STUART

www.roxtonfurniture.com
A solid-wood case goods manufacturer established in 1890, Roxton has three collections (the Heritage collection, the Turnbridge collection, and the Winchester Cherry collection), each with dining room, bedroom, occasional, home office, entertainment, and chairs plus lamps and accessories.

SEALY BEDDING AND MATTRESSES

www.sealy.com
If you factor in its subsidiaries, the Sealy Corporation is the largest bedding manufacturer in North America. The company produces a diversified line of mattresses and "foundations" (a.k.a. box springs) carefully designed for every body type and backache in the book. Sealy's bedding lines include Sealy, Sealy Posturepedic, Luxury Collection, Sealy Posturematic, and Sealy Kids. Sealy backs its reputation not only with statistics and claims but also puts its money where its mouth is and offers limited warranties on all its manufactured products—and it proudly claims the lowest consumer return rate in the bedding industry. Sealy warrants against manufacturing defects (e.g., broken or protruding coils or wires, extreme squeaks, rattles, or noises) and all currently manufactured Sealy Posturepedic models (and some other Sealy brand prod-

ucts) offer a ten-year "no-charge" warranty service period beginning on the date of purchase. The lengths of "no-charge" warranty periods vary from one to ten years on all of Sealy's other products. Pretty amazing when you consider just how much time the average person spends on a mattress.

SHERMAG, INC.

www.shermag.com

It's the wood glider rockers (wood with upholstered cushion seats and backs) with steel-encased ball-bearing mechanisms that really propelled this company into people's hearts. But there are plenty of other selections—bedroom, living room, home office, and youth furnishings—all in quality and all very stylish.

SHERRILL

www.sherrillfurniture.com

It isn't just the craftsmanship, tailoring, superior construction, and tradition that make Sherrill a standard within the industry, it's also the hands-on involvement of each and every craftsperson in the Sherrill factory that sets the standard that other manufacturers strive to meet. A distinguished name in upholstery, too, it is no surprise that whatever acquires the Sherrill label spells quality and style.

SPRING AIR

www.springair.com

It was 1926 when Francis Karr, the founder and visionary behind Spring Air, started the company and designed the free-end offset coil design, which adjusts to each sleeper's weight and is still the most copied design in the bedding industry to this day. Spring Air has continuously improved and evolved since that time and has emerged again and again with product improvements. In the late 1940's, the company introduced button-free technology. That was replaced with quilted surfaces (instead of fixing them with buttons) and extra-supportive bedding materials. In 1953, Spring Air began producing its Health Center mattress, which featured zones for different areas of the body. The company began manufacturing the Back Supporter mattress in the early 1960's, and sales doubled within seven years. Other revelations were the pillow-top mattress (1973), the Four Seasons concept (natural fiber bedding materials such as silk and wool, 1988), and Conforma foam which conforms to your neck, shoulders, and lower back (1991). In 1999, Spring Air introduced the ultra premium Back Supporter Comfort Caress collection, and in February 2001 Spring Air introduced the NeverTurn mattress feature with only one sleeping side—it never needs to be turned. The company is the fourth-largest bedding manufacturer in the world and still leads the industry in innovative product features and value.

STANLEY

www.stanleyfurniture.com
It was 1924 when young Thomas Bahnson Stanley embarked upon his dream to manufacture high-quality furniture at a price "the average American family could afford." Today Stanley Furniture Company is one of the largest, most recognized case goods manufacturers in the nation, and it still delivers on its original promise.

STATTON

www.statton.com
What started as a small manufacturer of bedroom furniture in 1926 has grown to become—more than 75 years later—a third-generation family owned and operated case goods man-

ufacturer with over 200 adapted and developed patterns in 18th- and 19th-century designs. Furnishings include bedroom, dining room, home office, occasional, wall systems, and even traditionally designed entertainment centers.

THAYER COGGIN

www.thayercoggin.com
Founded in 1953, Thayer Coggin was an early pioneer in contemporary upholstered furniture. Honored with the Outstanding Design Support Award by the American Society of Furniture Designers, Thayer Coggin continues to establish design trends and meet popular demand as is evidenced by its success not only in sales but also by the compliment of being exhibited locally in museums in North Carolina and farther afield in New York. Thayer Coggin includes myriad selections in contemporary styles for home and office: lounge chairs, sofas, dining chairs, recliners, modulars, and sectionals in all sorts of contemporary styles and designs.

THOMASVILLE

www.thomasville.com
Founded in 1904 as the Thomasville Chair Company, it wasn't until the 1960s that Thomasville was given its current name of Thomasville Furniture Industries. One of the most recognized names in furniture, Thomasville offers a full line of home furnishings in six lifestyle categories (Arts & Crafts, Earnest Hemingway, Cottage Casual, Traditional Elegance, Urban Perspectives, and Continental Influences) and 30 collections to suit every style and taste. It is important to note that Thomasville strictly enforces the policy that no customer may order Thomasville furnishings from a store that the customer has not visited within a set period of time. Thomasville also strictly enforces an MRP (Manufacturer's Retail Price), below which no authorized Thomasville retailer is allowed to sell

Thomasville products. Although this practice is objectionable, there is no denying the quality of Thomasville's products.

TROPITONE

www.tropitone.com

Award-winning quality casual outdoor furniture since 1954, Tropitone is built with a commitment to comfort, style, and value. Tropitone was the pioneer in the use of acrylic table-tops, wide aluminum extrusions (for arm comfort), and quick-drying, weather-resistant outdoor cushions. Tropitone offers lines in teak, cast aluminum and extruded aluminum, tailored cushions, straps, and slings so that you can customize your collection according to your comfort needs—and don't forget the Basta Sole Market Umbrella to complete the look.

TYNDALL CREEK

www.tyndallcreek.com

Solid wood casual comfort for outdoor, indoor, and "covered porch" furnishings, it's the rockers that set Tyndall Creek apart from the competition. Other products include bar stools, benches, and porch swings in choices of finishes and styles.

WEBB FURNITURE

www.webbfurn.com

A value-priced manufacturer of bedroom sets (in oak, cherry, and pine) and accent chests, Webb offers a variety of selections in traditional and transitional styles in an assortment of finishes.

WESLEY ALLEN

www.wesleyallen.com

Iron beds that "combine art and romance" are the Wesley Allen trademark. Beds in double, queen, and king—as well as twins with options like hideaways, trundles, and daybeds—will quickly become family favorites. Wesley Allen also produces a limited line of accessories.

WOODARD

www.woodard-furniture.com
Established in the 1930's, Woodard today continues the tradition of handcrafted wrought-iron furniture with the same attention to detail and craftsmanship implemented by its founder. Under the flagship Woodard brand, wrought iron, cast aluminum, and tubular aluminum products are manufactured using top materials and state-of-the-art finish systems for standard setting outdoor and casual furniture.

Appendix 2: Additional Online Resources

FURNITURE ASSOCIATIONS

American Furniture Manufacturers Association (AFMA): *www.afmahp.org*

American Society of Furniture Designers: *www.furninfo.com/associationasfd.html*

Hardwood Manufacturers Association: *www.hardwood.org*

Home Furnishings International Association (HFIA): *www.hfia.com*

National Home Furnishings Association (NHFA): *www.homefurnish.com/NHFA/home.htm*

Unfinished Furniture Association: *www.unfinishedfurniture.org*

Western Home Furnishings Association: *www.whfa.org*

Wood Products Manufacturers Association:
www.wpma.org

DESIGN ASSOCIATIONS

American Society of Interior Designers (ASID):
www.asid.org
Certified Interior Decorators International, Inc. (CID):
www.certifieddecorators.org
Interior Design Educators Council: *www.idec.org*
Interior Design Society (IDS):
www.interiordesignsociety.org
International Furnishings and Design Association
(IFDA): *www.ifda.com*
International Interior Design Association (IIDA):
www.iida.com
National Council for Interior Design Qualification
(NCIDQ): *www.ncidq.org*

MAGAZINES

Architectural Digest: *www.archdigest.com*
Better Homes & Gardens: *www.bhglive.com*
Furniture Magazine: *www.furnituremagazine.com*
Furniture Today: *www.furnituretoday.com*
Furniture World: *www.furninfo.com*
Martha Stewart's Living: *www.marthastewart.com*
Southern Living: *www.southernliving.com*
Traditional Home: *www.traditionalhome.com*
Upholster! Magazine Online: *www.upholster.com*
Upholstery Design and Manufacturing Online:
www.fdmmag.com/udmhome.htm

CONSUMER PROTECTION

Better Business Bureau: *www.bbb.org*

HIGH POINT, NORTH CAROLINA

Bienenstock Furniture Library: *www.furniturelibrary.com*

City of High Point: *www.high-point.net*

Furniture Discovery Center: *www.furniturediscovery.org*

High Point Chamber of Commerce: *www.highpointchamber.org*

High Point Convention & Visitors Bureau: *www.high-point.org*

High Point Economic Development Corp.: *www.high-point.net/dept/edc/index.htm*

High Point Museum: *www.highpointmuseum.org*

High Point Parks and Recreation Department: *www.high-point.net/dept/pr/*

High Point Public Library: *www.hipopl.org*

High Point University: *www.highpoint.edu*

International Home Furnishings Market (each April & October): *www.ihfc.com*

Millis Regional Health Education Center: *www.highpointregional.com*

North Carolina Furnishings Festival: *www.ncfurnishingsfestival.com*

North Carolina Shakespeare Festival: *www.ncshakes.org*

North Carolina Travel Information: *www.visitnc.com*

HICKORY, NORTH CAROLINA

Caldwell County Chamber of Commerce: *www.caldwellcochamber.org*

Catawba County: *www.co.catawba.nc.us*

Catawba County Chamber of Commerce: *www.catawbachamber.org*

Catawba County Council for the Arts: *www.charweb.org/arts/open/cccauaf1*

Catawba County Historical Association: *www.catawbahistory.org*

City of Hickory: *www.ci.hickory.nc.us*
Hickory Downtown Development Association:
 www.downtownhickory.com
Hickory Metro Convention Center:
 www.ci.hickory.nc.us/convention_center/
Hickory Museum of Art: *www.hickorymuseumofart.org*
Hickory Public Library: *www.ci.hickory.nc.us/library/*
Hickory Regional Airport: *www.ci.hickory.nc.us/airport*
Western Piedmont Symphony: *www.wpsymphony.org*

Glossary

The world of furniture has a language unto itself. Some terminology is unique to the business, while other words are familiar but used differently in the furniture business than they are in society at large. The following are some of the key terms you'll likely hear bandied about in North Carolina.

Accent Color
A highly visible, usually intense color used for contrast or pickup in a color scheme as a means of adding excitement.

Accessory
Nonfurniture items such as lamps, wall hangings, carpets, or other objects used in interior decorating.

Armoire
Traditionally kept in the bedroom, an armoire is a full-height enclosed cabinet used to store clothing. Many current designs can accommodate a television in the upper section with shelving or drawers below.

As is
Purchases from outlets are sold as is. In other words you're buying the furniture off the floor in its current condition and you have no recourse with the dealer or manufacturer once it leaves the store.

Bed
A bed in furniture language consists of a headboard, footboard, and rails, but not the box spring and mattress.

Biscuit Tufting

A method of tying back upholstery and padding (usually with upholstered buttons) to create square tufts on chair backs and seats.

Brand

The furniture's brand refers to the manufacturer of the furniture. A manufacturer may have several labels or lines.

Case goods

Wood furniture, typically dining rooms, bedroom sets, armoires, etc., as opposed to upholstered seating (couches, recliners, etc.).

China

The commonly used term for a breakfront or china cabinet.

C.O.D.

Cash on delivery. This means you pay when the shipment arrives, usually by certified check.

Collection

A line of furniture with certain attributes or design styles. A collection can also pertain to a line of furniture created in partnership between a manufacturer and a designer, retailer, or other well-known personality. (See Licensee.)

C.O.M.

Customer's own material. This means a piece of furniture will be upholstered with material provided by the customer.

Couch

A sofa or davenport.

Decorative

Describes furniture that adds beauty, not just function.

Depth of finish

Refers to the quality and appearance of the finish on wooden case goods.

Dovetail

A way of joining two pieces of wood together in, for example, a drawer. Wedge-shaped pieces on one piece of wood fit into similarly shaped notches in the other piece.

Considered a mark of quality.

Drop

A discontinued item, last year's line or design.

Dye lots

A quantity of fabric or leather that is dyed at one time with the same batch of dye. Even with the same color, batches vary from one lot to another depending on variables like humidity and weather.

Easy Chair

A big, comfortable, upholstered chair intended for relaxation. An easy chair can be in any style from any period.

Eight-Way Hand-Tied

A method of securing springs in upholstered seating. In an eight-way hand-tied piece, each spring is secured in eight different directions, giving exceptional strength and stability even in the event one or more ties become damaged. It is a mark of quality in seating, though not the only one (see photo).

Emboss

To decorate wood furniture with raised designs such as by stamping or pressing.

Ergonomics

Essentially, the science of comfort. An ergonomic chair, for example, is one specifically designed with the comfort of the human back and neck in mind.

Étagère

A cabinet with a set of open shelves for displaying small objects, sometimes with an enclosed cabinet as a base.

Finish

The color and processes applied to case goods, which will vary depending upon the run, the wood, and other factors like weather.

Fixed back

Nonremovable cushions or padding; in reference to the backing (where your back goes) on upholstered seating.

Frame

The underlying structure of a piece of furniture, as in the wooden frame (never seen) of a sofa.

French Chair

Upholstered chair used in England in the mid 18th century.

Gallery

A room or collection of rooms where furniture is showcased. A gallery might feature a single manufacturer's furniture or, alternatively, mix a number of manufacturer's furnishings together. Stores in the furniture malls (the Atrium Furniture Mall, Hickory Furniture Mart, and Catawba Furniture Mall) are often referred to as *Galleries*, *Showrooms*, and *Tenants*—each of which, in the text of this book, will be referred to as stores.

Grain

The alignment of fibers in wood, creating a directional pattern.

Hardware

The various handles, hinges, etc. on a piece of furniture.

Highboy

Traditionally, a tall chest—on legs—with four or five drawers.

Incliner

A tilt-back chair similar to a recliner but only the back goes down. Categorically also called motion furniture.

International Home Furnishings Market (known locally as "Market")

A twice-yearly furniture event which attracts retailers and designers from around the globe—there are attendees from all 50 states and 107 countries. It is the time when manufacturers are showcasing their new lines that will appear in stores 6 months down the line in North Carolina and closer to 8–12 months elsewhere in the country and the world. Market takes place every April and October in High Point. It is *not* open to the public. It is best to avoid shopping for furniture in North Carolina during these times because everyone who is anyone (and even those who aren't)—manufacturers, designers, sales personnel, florists, restaurants, hotels, you name it—are involved in Market. When in North Carolina and shopping for furniture, you will hear a lot of talk about Market. Attending Market makes the salespeople better informed (another way that shopping for furniture in North Carolina is superior to shopping at home: local salespeople attend Market each and every season whereas most furniture salespeople elsewhere in the country can't afford to attend or don't want to).

Joint fit

Case good furniture that is joined without nails.

K.D.

Knock-Down. Furniture that is shipped unassembled and put together upon arrival. See R.T.A.

Knockoff

A copy of another manufacturer's design.

Lathe

A machine that rapidly spins a piece of wood, such as a table leg, for carving and shaping purposes.

Licensee

A special brand-name collection produced by a manufacturer in conjunction with a designer, retailer or other well-known personality. Example: Lexington, the manufacturer, has licensed the Nautica brand name for a collection of furniture (Nautica Home). Other well-known licensees include Bob Timberlake, Robert Palmer (Palmer Home), Laura Ashley, and Ralph Lauren.

Long Clock

An 18th-century grandfather clock.

Loose back

Unattached cushions; in reference to the backing (where your back goes) on upholstered seating.

Love seat

A small sofa meant for two.

Manufacturer

Brand name or vendor. Also called a Line.

Market

(See International Home Furnishings Market.)

Matched

Furniture where the wood patterns are aligned and/or complementary; often referred to as matched or pattern-matched.

Motion furniture

Recliners, incliners. Comfort furniture—generally chairs and now sofas and sectionals—that recline.

M.R.P.

Manufacturer's Retail Price. The M.R.P. is the price set by the manufacturer, a price below which stores are not allowed to sell the manufacturer's first-quality products.

N.H.F.A.

National Home Furnishings Association.

Occasional

End tables, coffee tables.

Outlet

A clearance center where furniture is sold below the retail stores' prices. Outlet centers often carry scratch-and-dent pieces, previous season's designs, market samples, and so forth. An outlet store is what most people imagine when they think of furniture shopping in North Carolina though in fact, outlet business is minor in relation to that of the full-service retail stores that discount furniture prices.

Recliner

The quintessential comfort and relaxation chair (often associated with men and televised football games). The back goes down and the feet go up, though often either can be engaged without the other. Also called motion furniture.

R.T.A.

Ready to assemble. (See K.D.)

Run

Pieces produced together at one time under the same circumstances, with the same materials, dye, or finish—there might be 400–600 chairs in a run.

Scratch-and-dent

Damaged furniture.

Seating

Furniture that is covered in fabric or leather.

Showroom

Store.

Slipcover

A removable fitted cover that goes over the actual upholstery, for protection, to cover worn upholstery, or to provide variety.

Spindle

A slim rod, as on the back of some wooden chairs.

Tenant

A store in a mall.

Transitional

Furniture that is neither strictly traditional nor contemporary, often combining elements of both.

Trend

When certain design styles show up with a number of different manufacturers.

Turning

The carving and shaping of wood on a lathe.

Upholstery

Used colloquially to refer to the material (including leather) covering a sofa, chair, or ottoman, the term more precisely refers to the process of covering, padding, and stuffing upholstered furniture.

Velvet

The family of distinctive fabrics with a thick short pile and a smooth back. Velvet comes in a variety of configurations: plain, stripped, and figured, and is made from wool, silk, cotton, and synthetic fibers.

Veneer

A thin slice of attractive wood bonded to a less expensive piece of wood such as plywood or particle board for the purposes of making furniture look as though it is made of solid wood. Veneer has commonly achieved a negative connotation. But not all veneer is bad—many high-end manufacturers use veneers for intricately detailed wood surfaces.

Wholesaler

In the furniture business, the manufacturer is typically the wholesaler.

Index